BELLES OF LIBERTY

BELLES OF LIBERTY:

GENDER, BENNETT COLLEGE, AND THE CIVIL RIGHTS MOVEMENT IN GREENSBORO, NORTH CAROLINA

LINDA BEATRICE BROWN

Women and Wisdom Press
Greensboro, NC

Cover Photo:
Bennett Students: Sandra McBride, Mary Ellen Bender, and Others
Sit-In At Greensboro Lunch Counter
Photo: Courtesy of Bennett College Public Relations

Cover Design: Brandy Pickrell of Gloss Designs

Designed and Published by Women and Wisdom Press
A Creative Empowerment Project of Women and Wisdom Foundation

Women and Wisdom Press
Greensboro, NC

WWW.WOMENANDWISDOM.COM

ISBN 978-0-9888937-0-2
Printed in the United States of America

DEDICATION

This book is dedicated to all the Bennett women who
have accepted the call to witness, to stand for truth,
and to proclaim freedom to the captives of injustice.

*This is a Liberal Arts School where freedom
rings, so Martin Luther King can speak here!*
Dr. Willa Beatrice Player 1958

CONTENTS

FOREWORD

BY ESTHER ALEXANDER TERRY
BENNETT COLLEGE INTERIM PRESIDENT

James McMillan was professor of art at Bennett College during the years of the Sit-ins in Greensboro, North Carolina. In an interview that appears elsewhere in this book, Mr. Mac, as his students yet refer to him, recalls his own experiences as well as the role played by the women of Bennett in that historic movement for equal rights and human dignity. His penetrating summation that, "there ought to be a woman on that statue," gets immediately to the rationale for this book by Linda Brown.

The Greensboro Sit-ins are more than half a century past; and there is no one today who would deny the success of that movement in which women, men and children from the black community were joined by right-thinking people of other races in breaking down the barriers that had represented segregation and second-class citizenship to Black Americans in that city. Characterized by courage and revolutionary fervor, the Sit-in story is celebrated today by blacks and whites alike as a critical step in fulfilling the nation's promise of equality for all. It has found its way into countless libraries and museums; it appears in documentaries and is the subject of lectures throughout the nation and beyond. It is an heroic story that, as told, is the stuff of greatness: when four young black men ignore the deeply engrained cultural taboo against integrated eating facilities by sitting down at an all-White Woolworth lunch-counter in the

south, demanding to be served, they set off a civil rights movement that transformed the community. One might easily expect
that there is nothing left to do with this story except to celebrate
it as one of the many examples of the nation's confrontation with
itself over issues of civil rights that dominated the 1960s. Yet, an
unfortunate by-product of this otherwise heroic story calls us to
revisit it. Something about it will not let some of us rest.

The statue to which Mr. Mac refers is the one located on the
campus of North Carolina's A&T State University, a neighboring
institution with which the young women of Bennett College have
formed academic and social connections extending over many,
many years. The statue honors Ezell Blair, Franklin McCain,
Joseph McNeil and David Richmond who were, indeed, the first
to sit at the lunch-counter; in fact, they were the only ones to sit
down on February 1—a full day ahead of the others who
followed in the days afterward; and, because they were the first
to sit, they have been identified in the various publics as having
been "the leaders" of the movement, as if they acted
independently, without any connections to any others in the
community. This is what, even today, haunts most of the Sit-in
discussions by the women of Bennett College.

What is particularly troubling to many of those women,
particularly those who were students at Bennett and participated
in the Sit-ins, is that there has been little to no recognition of their
contributions. They insist that while what took place on February
1 is immeasurably significant as the first step in the carrying out
of the movement, the idea of the Sit-ins was not the brainchild of
the four young men exclusively, but an outgrowth of an action
that had been conceived and planned by a core group of students
and professors well before February 1,—a dedicated cadre that
included Bennett women as well as some A. & T. men. This
group, they hold, meeting often on Bennett's campus to plan and
strategize, provided the intellectual inspiration for the project;
this group was the backbone. Women, they contend, especially
the women of Bennett, have yet to receive proper credit for their

early, critical role in a movement that sent shockwaves through Greensboro and forever changed the way that city would do business; and until they have been duly credited, these women say, the story of the Woolworth Sit-in in Greensboro will be incomplete. "There ought to be a woman on that statue."

The good news for the readers of this book is that Linda Brown agreed to write it. Responding to the offer made to her by Dr. Julianne Malveaux, then president of the College, Ms. Brown acquiesced in the idea that she use some of her time as the Willa B. Player Distinguished Professor at Bennett to undertake the research that would allow her to write about the role of Bennett women in the Sit-ins. The result is this thoroughly documented book that I predict will be the instrument through which the women of Bennett, finally, will be able to see the fullness of their contributions acknowledged — more than fifty years later.

In several notable ways, Linda is uniquely qualified to have undertaken this project. For starters, she is an alumna whose student days at Bennett coincided with the first wave of the Sit-ins at the Woolworth lunch-counter; the fact of her presence at the action provides her with an unimpeachable perspective. But beyond her personal experience of the lunch-counter protests is the reality of her collegiate experience on the campus of Bennett College; her writing is benefitted by her having been subjected as a student to the College's philosophy of what an education in a young Bennett woman should look like. Nowhere on campus could she have turned to avoid the emphasis on Belle responsibility for the uplift of the community. She would have heard — many times over — the campus-wide praise for those Belles who, as far back as the 1930s had picketed in front of Carolina Theatre to protest the racist depictions of black people in such films as "Birth of a Nation"; and, if she herself did not participate in one of the most widely reported actions of her day, the College sponsored "Operation Door Knock", the largest voter registration drive that the community had seen up to that time, she was certainly on campus at the time that project was undertaken, and would have been able to escape the reports of the community's great pride in its success. Bennett Belles were educated with the expectation that they would reject and confront social injustice not only in their own lives, but wherever it manifested itself in the community. And Linda knows this better than any outside writer ever could. She brings this knowledge to her writing. Moreover, as the niece of Dr. Willa B. Player, president of the College during the period of the Sit-ins, Linda's access to her aunt's papers allows her to add a further dimension to the book in that she publicly presents, for the first time, something of Dr. Player's heroic stance in the backing and sustaining of "her girls" stalwart efforts.

It would have been enough had Linda chosen to write only what she knows about the Bennett experience and what she experienced personally of the movement, but, remarkably, she goes further. What she does not know and did not live, she turns to her Bennett Sisters, allowing their testimonies (one can actually hear them as voices) to augment her narrative. The result is a brilliant achievement: the recounting by a group of women — ensemble like, though independent of each other — of their Sit-in experiences (when they first began the protest, what propelled them, what they brought with them; what they took away; their fears, their joy) gives the book a rich tapestry, and the reader, palpable sense of what happened in Greensboro as having been a group experience, thus making it an incomparable witness.

Still, perhaps the greatest value of the book is that it provides a larger context for analyzing the under-recognition and the under-appreciation of the women's contribution to the Sit-ins. Setting her sights beyond the narrow confines of the city's history — and even beyond the turbulent era of 1960s, Linda urges us to look through the longer, dual lenses of U. S. race relations and its history of the treatment of women, to the probability that the myopic treatment of the Bennett women's work — its easy invisibility — is shaped by long legacies of chauvinism and racial intolerance that stretched back farther than the 1960s and wider than Greensboro and are even today not entirely absent from our culture: "Why [else] has it been so easy for the various writers about the Sit-Ins to ignore the black women participants"? "Why [else] has it not occurred to some of the writers about the movement to look beyond the actual act of the Sit-in on February 1 for a possible story leading up to that day"? And "why [else] did the one white Bennett student seated at the lunch counter draw so much more attention from the photographers than the black women seated alongside her? One Belle's astute analysis provides a historical context for our answers.

"There ought to be a woman on that statue" reflects Mr. Mac's desire to see public recognition of the courage with which the women of Bennett College, buoyed by their Bennett education, acted to confront the forces of their dehumanization, and how they were present from the very beginning. Mr. Mac is not alone. These were first class women, these Belles; their strong determination not to settle for second-class accommodations fired their courage and called them to action. Their story has not been told in its fullness — at least not until now. I am happy to commend this book by my classmate and friend as a most worthy witness to that valiant contribution to the making of a better America. Indeed, it is a special statue for my Sisters.

Esther Alexander Terry
Interim President
Bennett College

Acknowledgements

I am profoundly grateful to the many people who made this book possible, and without whom the work would never have been completed. Some projects seem to be divinely guided and meant to be, and many people are inspired to lend a helping hand. This was one of those projects. President Emerita Dr. Julianne Malveaux was the first to make it possible at Bennett College for me to begin the project. Interim President Esther Terry continued the institutional and personal support necessary for me to persevere and see the book into print. Without them it would still be a lovely idea but not a reality.

I am deeply appreciative to Women and Wisdom Foundation for the significant collaboration in facilitating the publication and distribution of the book. The gracious help of Diane Lamb at the *Greensboro News and Record* is greatly appreciated, as is the help of the Bennett College archival staff. Dr. William Chafe and Mr. Eugene Pfaff Jr. contributed untold richness to the study with their kind permission to use the interview material they had collected. Technical and graphic assistance was indispensible and I will ever be indebted to Barbara Tazewell, Diane Jones of Bennett College and especially Gabrielle Beard for their expertise and generosity. Many thanks to my husband for his support and encouragement. Finally of course I must thank my Bennett sisters who responded so eloquently when the call went out to contribute their words to our collective history, for without them, their courage and persistence in the face of all odds, there would be no story. And to all the Belles who gave of themselves for the cause of justice and freedom, my profound respect and thanks.

Deo Gratias,
Linda Beatrice Brown

INTRODUCTION

Tucked away in the northeastern corner of the city of Greensboro, NC, Bennett College's beautiful campus with its Georgian Colonial buildings, evokes tradition. It is a place where the "girls" were taught the finer things of life and the social graces. It appears to be the exact opposite of political activism and radicalism. These young women, often dressed in white and sheltered beneath magnolia trees, appear to have learned the lessons of gracious living associated with life in the American South. Bennett has been called "the Vassar of the South" for that reason.

Do not be misled. Oversimplification of this vision will leave you with exactly the wrong perception of the true genius that is Bennett College. There is another, more accurate way to understand what has gone on for 139 years in the halls of this liberal arts college for African American women.

The bell house at the right of the chapel holds a key to this puzzle. Inscribed on the bell are these words from Isaiah, verse 61:1 "....He hath sent me to bind up the brokenhearted, to proclaim liberty to the captives, and the opening of the prison to them that are bound."

This brings us to the reason for this book. Born in 1873, out of the trials of slavery and the struggle of emancipated slaves to become educated, the college chose a scriptural passage that perfectly reflects those times. American history teaches us that this was one of the most difficult periods in the country for African Americans, who were newly freed but constantly challenged by their circumstances, and challenged as well by many vengeful Whites who bitterly resented their loss of the war and the emancipation of blacks.

As the school built its strength and reputation, and changed to a liberal arts college for women, this impulse toward freedom and justice did not wane. The mission never truly changed. As I explained in *The Long Walk*, (82), the core of Bennett as we know it today had its beginnings in the leadership of Dr. David Jones, who became president in 1926 and was a courageous example of race leadership in the thirties and forties. Walking a difficult line between not offending White supporters and standing for social justice, he was known to be unyielding when it came to his principled decisions. Willa Player, who was mentored by Dr. Jones, and followed him as president, said, "I don't think Dr. Jones was ever anybody to do anything other than what he thought was right" (Pfaff, Player interview 23).

Hobart Jarrett, professor during Jones's presidency and beyond, goes further than that.

> *Chafe: Was Dr. Jones ever discouraged?*
>
> *Jarrett: Anything other than that. Jones brought Eleanor Roosevelt to Bennett…and he insisted that Mrs. Roosevelt speak in Bennett's chapel and he opened the doors. It was the only integrated place in the whole city, no question about that, none whatsoever. Anybody that says anything different is wrong. Woman's College, no. A&T College, hell, no. Bennett had several White faculty people. And Bennett had [White] exchange students between our college and another. We had one White girl while I was there who had come as an exchange student and she graduated….Bennett was a fighting institution." (Chafe, Jarrett interview, Civilrightsgreensboro.library.uncg.edu).*

Dr. Jones died in 1955, but the ground had been laid for the movement that was soon to hit the Bennett College campus. Already the revolution in race relations had begun with the Montgomery Bus Boycott that same year. There is no doubt that Willa Player, the next president of Bennett, was greatly inspired by Dr. Jones and she continued many of the precedents set by her predecessor. At a service held in memory of Dr. Jones, in 1961, Dr. Peter Murray, the speaker, said, "Dr. Jones hated second class citizenship with every fiber of his being. If he were alive today he would be proud to associate himself with all those fighters of intolerance wherever it raised its ugly head" (*Greensboro Daily News* 16 Jan 1961 A4). Dr. Player is remembered for her courageous stands during this period, including her decision to allow Dr. Martin Luther King to speak on the campus in 1958. She was willing to take a stand in spite of whatever the city of Greensboro thought. Player knew the controversial nature of her decision. "Bennett is a liberal arts college where freedom rings so Martin Luther King can speak here," she said, after all of the institutions in the city had denied him access.

In 1959 it came as no surprise to the Rev. John Hatchett of the Bennett faculty that Player would support the organizing meetings he held with Bennett students, planning the Sit-ins. He was not in fear of his job and was very honest with her about the agenda for those meetings. He knew that his president would support his actions and those of his students. It was the logical culmination of the institutional philosophy that was evident at Bennett.

Research on the 60's period is abundant. A glance at the existing movement scholarship reveals its fascination for scholars. So why do we need another book about the Sit-ins? Perspective is everything in the interpretation of history.

"History is written by the winners" is not an idle statement. In the case of the story of the Greensboro Sit-ins, it is the winners' story that is not complete, if we choose to call those

Americans who were demonstrating for their civil rights "winners".

For many years questions have been raised that have to do with who started the Sit-ins in Greensboro. Before I go further, let me say that this is not a book that argues about who started the movement in Greensboro. That is a waste of time and reduces the scholarly conversation about this movement to the "he said, she said" level. There are many good reasons that the story of the Greensboro Four has gone into myth and legend. I am using the word myth here to refer to the cultural stories that are "sacred" to communities – the stories we tell ourselves about ourselves. This story is part of the lore of this medium sized Southern city that became nationally known as a result of its Black citizens' attempts to break down the old segregated pattern, a legacy of slavery. As history moves forward we uncover pieces of the story that add to the legend. Myth and legend are powerful forces. We need myth and legend because we need to understand our own stories and to be inspired by them. Sometimes, news in the media becomes legend or myth and moves into the history books. Numerous scholars are aware that the participation of women in the national Civil Rights Movement was a key to its success. The same is true of the Greensboro movement. It is my intention here to examine the role of Bennett College women in particular within this legend that is Greensboro's story. I hope to add one more voice to that piece of the historical narrative of Greensboro.

In this work we will consider the impact that gender had on the extraordinary events that are celebrated as "the Greensboro Sit-ins in 1960" and the role of Bennett women. Also we will consider the role of gender and Bennett women in the following Civil Rights Movement in Greensboro. The movement to desegregate public accommodations in the city immediately followed the Sit-ins there and lasted from 1961 to 1963. We will try to understand this in a larger context also, and make comparisons of Bennett women with women activists nationally for the role of women activists all over the country was a major factor in the success of the movement. Considerable work has been done on this latter topic, including *Gender and the Civil Rights Movement* by Peter J. Ling and Sharon Monteith, first published in 1999.

The Greensboro Sit-ins have been oversimplified, like much of the history surrounding the Civil Rights Movement. The Rosa Parks story is an example. There was planning in Montgomery, and a support system that we seldom hear about. There were at least three attempts by women to integrate the buses before Rosa Parks. In Montgomery, Jo Ann Robinson had tried to take a seat in front of the bus in 1949. For various reasons, however, Parks became the symbolic "first." In popular culture it is effective to tell the stories of heroic acts as dramatically as possible, especially in the media. The groundwork gets lost in the sensationalism of the dramatic acts that remain in the memory of most people. Similarly, no movement is simply begun by four people, but grows out of very tangled threads of human experience. What we must remember is that many, many people contributed to the independent action that was taken by the courageous young men of A&T State University before that action was ever attempted.

History is composed of fragments of information, scraps of memory, records of facts, documents, voices, clippings, and photographs which taken together make up what comes to be known as history.

"I was there. I know." This is the voice of the eyewitness. This voice is sometimes believed, sometimes not. This voice is sometimes denied due to the unreliability of the witness, the prejudice of the witness, or because the recorder has ulterior motives. Consequently history is basically unreliable no matter how carefully documented, for the human factor is fallible, flawed and often prejudiced. At best there are many different versions of the truth as we know it. Think about it. Would General Grant's version of the Civil War be the same as Robert E.

Lee's? Would an African captive on a slave ship tell the same version as the slave catcher on that same ship? And yet they could both say "I was there. I know what happened."

It has been noted by numerous scholars that there are reasons for the partial "invisibility" of women activists in the Civil Rights Movement. A few Greensboro citizens have recently admitted to me that they have limited awareness of Bennett's involvement in the Greensboro movement, even though this participation has been duly noted by William Chafe in his 1981 work, *Civilities and Civil Rights*. Apparently the popular conception in the city has been that the demonstrations were principally an A&T State University "thing."

We know, as archeologists do, that there are layers and layers of experience waiting to be uncovered. But we are even further from the truth when major pieces of the historical fabric are missing. Until these layers of history are made visible the story will remain incomplete. The narrative in the International Civil Rights Museum in downtown Greensboro only briefly mentions Bennett College women along with the women of Greensboro College and UNC-G (formerly Woman's College) and effectively relegates Bennett's role to an interesting footnote.

This book represents an attempt to answer questions, specifically about Bennett College and its role in the push for justice and desegregation of all of Greensboro's public accommodations. What role did Bennett College women play in the two major periods of civil rights demonstrations during 1960 and 1961-63? Why has there been a minimum of recognition for the Bennett contribution to the movement in Greensboro? What is the role of cultural and gender norms in the "invisibility" of Bennett College women? In what way did the women of Bennett College make a major contribution to the opening of Greensboro? How and why did they do so? How did their participation reflect the mission of the College? What patterns in the national Civil Rights movement can we see repeated in the response to the participation of Bennett College women? Are there conclusions we can draw that will help complete the story of women activists who were instrumental in changing the United States of America in the years of the non-violent passive resistance push for equality?

To this end we will take a brief look at some of the studies that have been done regarding women activists in this era; we will look at Bennett College as an institution that nurtured and supported this activism, and we will listen to some of the voices of those Bennett Women who were involved in the demonstrations, as they tell their stories.

History is a story we tell ourselves about ourselves. As such it is a powerful key to our collective destiny. We hope that we can add to the totality and truth of the story, because it is the story that empowers, that tells us who we are, and affirms us.

Gender dynamics are never removed from human history. Young people in this generation see the Civil Rights Movement almost as far removed from themselves as the Civil War. Young women should know and be proud of their power. That is one way we proclaim liberty to the captives. As Black women we are keenly aware of the impact of misogyny, both historically and in the present. The trivialization of women's stories is one result of misogyny. Young Black women need their stories, as do all women, because our history, or should I say, "herstory," is critically important to who we are and who we will become; hence it is seriously important to the future of our world. Furthermore we seek to give the story of Bennett the place it deserves in history to firmly place it in the "sacred story" that is central to Greensboro's identity. It is a key to the history and character of the city.

In this time of extreme cynicism and loss of hope, the election of President Obama raised hopes that could not be fulfilled in the short time of four years, and these hopes have been sabotaged at every turn. The future of our country and indeed of the world, really depends on the development of a generation of young people who have a vision that is fueled by the certainty that it is possible for us to live together as human beings in peace, and that is it is possible for all of us to have access to opportunity and respect for each other. The young people of the sixties movement, those who sat down in Greensboro, those who marched and went to jail with so much hope in possibility, the women of Bennett College who made the decision to lift the veil of female respectability and step out into history deserve to be remembered; but more than that, they are greatly needed today. Their story must be told. We have need of the example of their courage, their vision and their absolute certainty that there was a better way. If their story is lost we are the poorer for it, and so much further behind than ever. If their story is not told, our own young women and men will not have that powerful inspiration they need to go forward on their own journey of faith to make the world a better place. It is as important to remember them as it is to remember Dr. King, for without them and others like them nothing would have changed. We are no longer captive to the laws of segregation. We are captive to our own hopelessness and immobility. We must tell the story to the grownups lest they fall captive to the despair that comes of giving up. We must tell the story to the young, lest they fall captive to the belief that hatred and intolerance, poverty, and war are "normal" and there is no other way to live. We must "proclaim liberty to the captives and the opening of the prison to them that are bound." To that end, this is our story.

Linda Beatrice Brown
Bennett College
Greensboro, North Carolina
March 2013

Chapter 1

The Beginning

"Martin Luther King can speak here."
Willa B. Player

They walked the campus, students and faculty, staff and sometimes parents, enjoying the ambiance of gracious Southern living, African American style, not knowing that the year 1958 would bring history squarely into the center of the college quad. The day we heard Dr. Martin Luther King was going to speak on our campus the rest of Greensboro also knew it. They also knew that Dr. King had led a boycott of the Montgomery bus system in 1955 to 1956, encouraging Black domestic workers to walk to work rather than sit in the backs of busses that took them to clean and cook for the White families of their city. And as such, he was not just controversial, but was considered dangerous by many to have a public gathering at which he appeared. The visit of Dr. King to Bennett was not without a context of risk and the threat of possible violence. In 1957 President Eisenhower had signed into law the first civil rights bill since Reconstruction about voting rights. In 1955 Rosa Parks had been arrested and jailed. In 1954 Emmett Till had been brutally murdered, and Brown VS the Board of Education had ruled school segregation unconstitutional, and in 1957, Little Rock Arkansas had exploded with Black students' attempt to integrate Central High School. There was an intense climate in the entire country at that time which made Player's decision to invite Dr. King to the campus vibrate with importance and courage.

The presidents of the other four colleges and universities in town all the churches Black and White, and all other agencies had refused the NAACP's request for a venue for Dr. King. They had not figured on Willa Player, the president of Bennett College. As the successor to Dr. David D. Jones who died in 1955, Dr. Player had been mentored by a principled and stubborn leader who refused to back down when challenged about his invitation to Mrs. Franklin D. Roosevelt in the 40's. He insisted on an integrated audience for her in the college chapel. He refused to have any but Black contractors to build his buildings. He had given permission for his daughter to lead a boycott of Greensboro theaters in 1937 by Bennett students when it was found that the movies were being doctored to omit positive images of Blacks. This is the man who had tutored Willa Player and she had sat at his knee and listened, and this is why she decided that King should speak on the campus in spite of the risks.

The soft-spoken president of Bennett College gave one of her most powerful speeches in May of 1958. She was the keynote speaker at the Fifth Assembly of the Women's Society of Christian Service of the Methodist Church and the speech was entitled "Our Witness". It is an address that calls on the women of Methodism, indeed of the Methodist church itself, to give authentic Christian witness by making available equality of access to all institutions of Methodist Christian education. The speech is aggressive in its unequivocal stance against segregation. The leader of the "Belles" who would eventually help to fill the jails of Greensboro reveals clearly the reason that these college women felt entirely supported by their president.

> *Our institutions in the home field stand to lose their Christian influence. As long as there is one among us who*

lacks the courage of the conviction to open the door to all students who thirst for knowledge, whether this be a kindergarten, a settlement house, a secondary school, a college, a theological seminary, or a university center. Our witness is weakened whenever the search for truth is hampered by policies or procedures that separate our minds by false or arbitrary identifications. If we be witnesses we are called to rise above our fears, the ambitions, the bigotry and the tensions of a culture beset with controversy, in total acceptance of our God-given right and responsibility to pass on love and learning to teach new generations as true servants of God having been chosen to fulfill his purpose among men (Player papers, 1958).

Perhaps King had added fire to her already strong convictions. The evening of Dr. King's visit was mild for February 11. Yet the South could be deceptively inviting. On Bennett's campus, the chapel, the theater, and Black Hall assembly were all full to overflowing with students, faculty and with Greensboro citizens, sitting everywhere to get a glimpse of this now famous (infamous to some) man who was beginning to form his historical destiny as the leader of "the dream."

Prior to the evening, he was interviewed by student reporters from the *Bennett Banner*. They did not know that his visit would be part of their contribution to history as well, which would come two years later almost to the day, February 1, 1960, when they would become a part of the historic Sit-in movement.

Dr. King does not mince words with the students as he answers their questions. When they ask him what was his greatest moment of fear he answers that it was January of 1956 when he was getting thirty or forty threats a day during the boycott in Montgomery.

He talks about the murder of Till and the castration of an innocent man from Birmingham. Prophetically, he tells them that the people he's working with are starting a voting crusade. The

Bennett College voter registration project "Operation Door Knock" would come in 1960 and would register more people than ever before in Greensboro. King talks to the students about Little Rock: "These nine children who have gone to Central High need the greatest commendation and praise for their ability to stand with so much dignity amid such tragic, not only intimidation but harassments and actual violence because many of them faced violence. The fact that these little, these young people could stand up with so much courage and yet so much dignity in the midst of all the abuses that they've had to confront". (*Interview at Bennett, MLK-kppo1 Stanford.edu, Feb. 1958*).

There is no way to measure Dr. King's affect on the Bennett reporters that afternoon. It is hard to imagine that being in Dr. King's presence and hearing his passion would not have impressed these young people who went that evening to hear his speech, or when they made the decisions they made two years later to Sit-in and march. We do know that many of the Greensboro movement's participants say Dr. King was an inspiration and that his visit was very important to them.

That night there were Greensboro citizens standing outside Annie Merner Pfeiffer Chapel and speakers were set so that the public without seats could hear what this incredibly inspiring orator had to say. As Dr. King's unforgettable voice rang out in the packed chapel, he reminded his audience that everyone's contribution to the achievement of civil rights is valuable. No matter how insignificant they are, the "ground crew" are those who get every plane off the ground. He could not have known that many of the students and citizens sitting in the chapel would soon join the "ground crew" of the Sit-ins and the Civil Rights Movement in Greensboro.

CHAPTER 2

THE RESPECTABILITY FACTOR

*"The second great step to creative living is a burning
desire to be somebody out of the ordinary."*
Benjamin Mays in the Bennett Chapel

It is a Sunday afternoon in March 1958 on the campus of
Bennett College. The campus bell has rung out and the "young
ladies exit the residence halls walking fast, so as not to be late to
vespers. Being tardy to chapel is unthinkable on any day, and
this afternoon the vespers speaker is Dr. Benjamin E. Mays, the
President of Morehouse College.

Bennett women are dressed as if for church, decked in hats
gloves, heels and stockings, required dress for chapel. The
college choir is already lined up in the vestibule in their
burgundy cassocks and carefully pressed white surplices, and
black flats all alike.

This scene, as well as any depicts the emphasis placed on
correct deportment, dress and lady-like respectability that was
de rigueur on the campus in those days, and had been since the
conception of the college for women.

"The Bennett Way of Life," while at its center had placed a
strong emphasis on scholarship and leadership, also placed a

high priority on respectable lady-like behavior. Player writes in *The Art of Living at Bennett College*, (the handbook for entering freshmen), "Bennett students are expected to conduct themselves at all times in the restrained and distinctive manner which should characterize the behavior of young women."

Restraint and dignity were associated with any woman who went through the Bennett education, the habits of four years of conditioning and expectation. The College took seriously its responsibility to prepare the young women for life in a hostile environment where race would be a major factor in their chances for success. The classes in correct etiquette, how to set a table, host an event, dress and behave at receptions looked forward to a new world for these young women. It would be a world of expanding career opportunities and these young women would be in positions where they needed to be prepared for competing in settings many of them were not used to, and as citizens in a desegregated world. The Bennett way of life recognized the pressures of racial judgment which they would confront as soon as graduation was over.

This emphasis on respectability can be seen in Black middle class life nationally and permeates the strategy of the Civil Rights Movement, especially in the earlier days of the movement. There was definitely a use for this tactic. Black Americans hoped to avoid the worst of White racism by adopting what passed as "White" ideals of respectability. After all, they had been called savages during the horrific days of Reconstruction and the resultant Jim Crow laws played on the fears of many Whites that Blacks had to be controlled, lest they get out of hand and revert to their "African savagery". Black women had been subject to the stereotypes of "the Jezebel," a loose woman who was sexually promiscuous and immoral by nature. And so in the 50's and 60's, the Southern Civil Rights Movement extended and refined the idea of Black respectability. According to Marisa

Chappell,[1] this provided the movement with an important antidote to the claims of Southern Whites that they had to protect American civilization from uncivilized Blacks with their "congenital ignorance, sloth, promiscuity and irresponsibility". By the 1950's respectability was a genuinely internalized value for most African Americans, especially in the growing middle class.

The Black freedom fighter would appeal to mainstream America by presenting "perfectly coiffured, immaculately dressed, quietly dignified and stoically non-violent black demonstrators" (Chappell, p. 69). An image of women who were morally virtuous, properly dressed and restrained in behavior was part of a strategy for garnering support and presenting an ironic contrast to the stereotypes that had been used against us. Jibreel Khazan (who was known as Ezell Blair at the time) was one of the original four A&T State University students who sat in. He had the following to say about Willa Player and her behavior during the Greensboro Sit-ins. What he calls feminine is a way of referring to her image, which at the time, was that of the epitome of lady-like respectability:

> There was Dr. Willa Player at Bennett College. She was always feminine. But she was also liberated. And she was not afraid to take a stand. She told the managers of Woolworth and Kress and the city officials when we met Friday night February 5 that she was backing the students to the hilt. She said 'these students are only fulfilling the rights spoken of in the Constitution of the United States and also being good religious people what was in the Bible'. You should have seen the smiles that we broke into when we looked at each other and said 'that's telling them' (Pfaff, Jibreel Khazan interview, 107).

---

[1] See Chappell, Marisa et. al. in Ling, Peter J. *Gender and the Civil Rights Movement* 72.

Elizabeth Betsy Toth was one of the White students who joined the Bennett women at the lunch counter. She experienced the deep conviction on the part of the Bennett women that respectability was part of the strategy of the movement:

> Sitting to my right were a bunch of Bennett ladies who were so much more well behaved than I was. They were dressed better. Their deportment was better. They were the ones who taught me how to do this right. A couple of times I was about to go after the woman who was threatening to hit me. That's when the ladies from Bennett said:"
>
> 'No you're not.' One said, 'Honey if you ever look like you're going to do that we are quits with you. You're out of here. We do not need that....That will not work....I don't care if she does hit you. You do nothing. You learn to do nothing. You just sit and be. And you conduct yourself with dignity and quiet.' So in my one day I learned my civil rights behavior. The ladies from Bennett had it down. They were the best. (Pfaff, Toth interview, 97).

This is the learned behavior that was behind the Way of Life at Bennett and that was much older than the Sit-in Movement. As we shall see it was strongly connected to survival and coping mechanisms in the Black community.

Listen to the words of Dr. Benjamin Mays, President of Morehouse College (An African American College for men), speaking in the chapel to Bennett students on that day in March, 1958:

> Anybody can be nothing. Anybody can gamble, get drunk; anybody can become a drug addict; anybody can be lazy, trifling, good for nothing; anybody can be nobody. The second great step to creative living is a burning desire to be somebody out of the ordinary. (Mays, "Creative Living for Youth in a Time of Crisis," The Bennett College Social Justice Lecture Series, 23).

Partly as a result of the heavy Victorian message to women that was still very much alive in 1958 (we were, after all, only 58 years away from the turn of the century) respectability for women was a major requirement in the struggle for civil rights. Moral virtue provided some protection against the inevitable backlash from Whites. When asked why the Bennett women had to wear hats and gloves, Willa Player answered that it was to keep White people from treating the Bennett students with the casual disdain and disrespect they would be subject to if seen as less than college girls. Once the Bennett women were arrested in the protest movement, one of the prison guards had said "I thought you girls had class but you don't. You don't know your place."

"The cult of true womanhood" of the previous century had set a standard that White society used to define the acceptability of its female members. The virtuous woman was taught to be a pillar of morality, in addition to being submissive to her husband, devoted to the home, but never active in the world. The mentality of "the woman's place" was still very much alive in the 1950's, especially in the Southern way of life. Women were the embodiment of all that was refined in civilization.

All of this notwithstanding, fifty years into the century the women activists of the Civil Rights Movement were not just needed but were indispensable to the progress of civil rights. They pushed the envelope of gender roles by demonstrating, marching and going to jail for civil rights. The country had seen this earlier in the struggle to give women the vote, when the reaction of many was scorn and violent treatment, including incarceration for White women who dared to step outside the confines of their "place."

Rosa Parks is an example of the need for a "respectable" image of womanhood in the movement. According to Chappell and others, Rosa Parks was a trained political activist who fit the movement's need during the Montgomery Bus Boycott for a respectable female symbol. "In the construction of Parks' public image as a symbol, leaders of the protest and the Black press insistently downplayed her activist credentials in favor of an emphasis on her middle class morality and femininity revealing how deeply these notions had penetrated mass Black consciousness" (Chappell, 83).

Respectability and invisibility or marginalization of women worked hand in hand to influence the roles women were allowed to play in the Movement and the effacement that was the result. This traditional subordinate role was a national phenomenon. In the Black press, Black women were told to examine themselves for the cause of their man's infidelity and to give up their careers for their men. Black men were supposed to emphasize the role of head of the family and de-emphasize the hyper sexuality of the stereotype of Black men. *Tan* magazine advised women to take "prime responsibility for a successful relationship or marriage". The Black press endorsed patriarchal authority and consigned women to traditional roles, placing this within the code of respectability (Chappell, 75).

In order to reinforce Park's image of unassailable respectability, movement leaders and the Black press rarely mentioned her involvement with the NAACP or Highlander School in Tennessee, with its devotion to education for progressive causes. Martin Luther King appeared to distance Parks from her own history of political engagement. The Black press neglected the more radical implications of mass Black female insurgency, (the bus boycott), in favor of an emphasis on middle class propriety and domesticity. One Black newspaper described Parks as "retiring and perfectly poised and noted that she doesn't appear to fit the role in which she is now cast." Various publications refer to her as "soft spoken," "quiet and refined" (Chappell, 89).

In the light of the country's emphasis on the proper female role, Parks' action was interpreted as one of racial defiance, not gender defiance. However, in truth it was both. The woman's place was clearly not in the streets getting arrested for breaking the law. The same was true of the Bennett women whose participation was seen as taking a stand for racial justice, which of course it was, not breaking gender mores, which it also was. Their gender is also the reason the participation of Bennett women was nearly invisible in the popular perception and neglected in the scholarly ranks, until the work of Isaacs in 2002 and Flowers in 2005. Barbara Isaacs' dissertation, *The Lunch Counter Struggle 1960-1963: Women Remapping Boundaries of Race Gender and Vocation* is a major contribution. Her careful scholarship makes available an analysis of Bennett's role in the Sit-ins vis-à-vis the Methodist Church's connection to the College.

Deidre Flowers also does seminal work in her 2005 article, *"The Launching of the Student Sit-In Movement: The Role of Black Women at Bennett College."* Flowers highlights the important role of Bennett College students and Willa Player in the Greensboro Sit-ins and gives the names of 10 students who were among those from Bennett arrested on April 22, 1960. The list is not exhaustive.

Gender and the Civil Rights Movement, edited by Peter Ling and Sharon Monteith et. al., totally omits Bennett College and Willa Player. Miles Wolff's book, *Lunch at the 5 & 10,* first published in 1970, puts a great deal of emphasis on the fact there were two White students from Bennett who participated as well as White women from Woman's College (now UNC-G). He mentions that these girls were arrested along with "Black students." There is no mention that many of these women were from Bennett College. Wolff mentions that Bennett women were present at the counter by February 3. He goes on to make note of the guest speakers who were at Bennett that spring, including Thurgood Marshall and Frederick Patterson, and the leadership of Hobart Jarrett, Bennett faculty member. Wolff observes that: "virtually the whole student bodies of A&T and Bennett were willing to come and take part" (50). However, we are not told how he knows this. Willa Player gets one brief nod as having attended a meeting on February 5 with other educators and business leaders.

William Chafe's, *Civilities and Civil Rights* does not give us a gendered analysis of Bennett's role, but one gets a more balanced view of the activities of Bennett women and their president. He gives some important background on the history of political activism of Bennett also, saying: "Bennett in particular, stood forth as a model of racial strength" (p. 26). We shall see how the idea of respectability combined with cultural habit of effacement of women to produce a kind of amnesia regarding the Bennett College role in Greensboro.

It is not only the simple need to counter the stereotyping of women as Jezebels that made respectability an important factor in the freedom struggle. It is much more complicated than that. Danielle L. McGuire chronicles several cases of the rape of Black women by White men in the 40's and 50's. In the disturbing case of Florida A&M coed Betty Jean Owens, who was kidnapped and gang raped, McGuire explains the depth of the need felt by civil rights activists, both men and women, to utilize "the politics of respectability". "Respectability became the key to Black women's symbolic place in the Civil Rights Movement in the early 1950's" (McGuire, 914).

In the Deep South especially, there was a climate of violence against almost any attempt by Blacks to rewrite the racial story of America. McGuire reminds us that the White Citizens Council and others relied heavily on sexual scare tactics and White fears of racial mixing and miscegenation. Any impropriety on the part of African Americans could be interpreted as threatening the social order (McGuire, 913).

Ironically the brutal rape of Betty Owens was used to fuel fears of the "Black male beast," the stereotyped brute attacking White women, as iconically seen in the movie "Birth of a Nation." Fears that reprisals by Black men would be the result of the conviction of Owen's rapists were played upon.

The courageous testimony of Betty Jean Owens in a courtroom with her attackers broke the silence of dissemblance that Black women had often practiced as a tactic of survival. Her middle class background, her education, her chastity no doubt gave more weight to her national and local supporters and enabled the verdict of guilty for her attackers. Respectability as a factor in the struggle for racial justice involves the deep-seated sexual/racial pathology that has always been a part of the racist dynamic in America. This was well understood by leading Black writers, James Baldwin and Ralph Ellison, as seen in their works.

The racial history of the sexual abuse, violence and exploitation of Black women is one area of analysis and exploration that deserves more study and exploration. As McGuire says: "if we are to fully understand the role of gender and sexuality in larger struggles for freedom and equality we must explore these battles over manhood and womanhood, frequently set in the context of sexualized violence that remain at the volatile core of the modern Civil Rights Movement" (93).

In other words, Betty Jean Owen's horrific experience was not an aberration but an integral part of the story of racism in America, and one in a long line of outrageous violent acts against Black women. Seen in this light, respectability as a tactic becomes much more than a useful tool. It is an answer to the hate filled campaign of terrorism that is over 300 years old.[2]

Thus we must look at the use of respectability from a multi-layered perspective. For African American freedom fighters, both men and women, understanding the necessity of not handing their enemies and detractors any more ammunition than they already had or could fabricate was crucial. Combined with that was the sincere belief on the part of many Black men that the traditional female role was the right one, sanctioned by the Bible, societal norms and cultural tradition. In addition to this powerful mix is the human factor of Black men whose

---

[2] It is for this reason that the author feels that the novel and movie, *The Help*, is more than a little unrealistic. The domestic help, left behind to cope with the fallout of their exposure of racism in Mississippi, would certainly not have been able to walk peacefully away from their acts of defiance, but would have paid dearly.

masculinity has been psychologically assailed, and the object of murderous and violent assault during and since slavery. Thus, respectability partners with the need to keep women marginal, and sometimes nearly invisible for their protection, and for the sake of keeping intact the fragile Black male identity that is the result of racist domination.   Therefore, in many ways the presence of Black women activists in the Civil Rights struggle has been trivialized and marginalized and we will take a look at how the phenomenon of invisibility has applied to the Greensboro movement.

CHAPTER 3

"LIFTING THE VEIL"

*"It is indefensible to call a national march and not send out a
call which contains the name of not one single woman leader."*
Dr. Pauli Murray

It is February 3, 1960 in Greensboro, NC. A young woman
dresses carefully to go to her class at Bennett College. She
chooses a skirt and blouse, bobby socks and "penny" loafers. She
knows that slacks are only allowed on Saturday afternoon and
she has somewhere to go after class. She picks up her coat
against the February chill and her books to take to class,
choosing carefully, since one of them will have to be for extra
reading today. And then she hesitates. What else would she need
that afternoon? What if they were arrested? The thought was
frightening but she had made up her mind.

Crossing the Bennett College quadrangle her mind was only
divided about her studies and the time she was giving to the Sit-
in project. She wondered how long this would go on and how
much time she could afford to lose from class? What they were
doing was dangerous but she quickly blocked that out of her
mind. Gloria had gone to town yesterday, the first Bennett

woman to do so. The morning flew by and in a wink of an eye it was time to meet the others. They were to meet outside the student union. It was, she thought, the right thing to do. It was what her parents and her professors had taught her, to stand up for what was right. It had to be done. There was a car full. Another car had gone ahead already. As she got into the car she prayed and suggested that the others do so. Her classmates were silent, lost in their own thoughts. Downtown was two minutes away from the campus. There was no time to hesitate. A car full of coeds with colorful skirts and bobby socks, their hair carefully combed, emptied onto the sidewalk. All had brought books to study. Somebody said, "Walk this way," and they followed, filing into Woolworth toward the empty seats and the young Black men who were sitting in. The store was not empty; it was full of curious onlookers, mostly White, and some who looked hostile and threatening. Some of them yelled threatening and ugly words.

They slipped into their seats silently. No one spoke. Their allotted time was one hour, the student leader had said. Someone would relieve them in one hour. A White waitress walked by without asking, "can I help you," and the student didn't look up. Finally she looked up into the eyes of the waitress who was carrying a tray of knives. The knives were rattling because the waitress's hands were shaking. She looks afraid too, the student thought. She finished her assigned hour, reading but not remembering anything she read. It was time to go.

They moved all at once and left the store aware that the fellows from A&T College were watching out for them on the street corners. They were spotting potential trouble-makers who yelled obscenities as they walked out of the five and dime, proud of what they had done. A little giddy, a little nervous but excited about the demonstration, they walked onto their nearby campus completely unaware that they were part of a February in Greensboro that would change, not just Greensboro, but the world.

The Bennett student who started her day by going to class did not know that she had become a symbol for the entire world, a symbol of all those earnest young college students in America who believed there was a better and more just way to live. She had no way of knowing that one day two years later at least half the student body of Bennett College would eventually be jailed for the stand they were taking on desegregation of Greensboro. So much would happen in the weeks and months to come. Life in America would literally be changed forever.

It is, of course, not factual to say that the Bennett women have been entirely erased from the historical record. But it is accurate to say that their participation has been for a long time played down and unnoted in much writing about the movement, and in the Greensboro popular conception of what happened. The typical retelling and hence the typical image of what happened in those early days in Greensboro has been very short on Bennett's important role.

It is simply that the traditional "place" of African American women in the Black community made the male privilege of taking "first place" a comfortable, easy, and acceptable thing to do. When this phenomenon is understood in its complexity it should answer some important questions about our history as Black women and men.

Our aim is to lift the veil of invisibility so that the role of our activist sisters is more accurately seen and understood. In reviewing the lack of visibility of the Bennett contribution, we must not fall into the blaming game, but we do need to say that the marginalization has been there and that Bennett College shares with many other civil rights sisters this phenomenon of effacement. In other words, there is a national pattern here, whether through habit or on purpose, of overlooking the contributions, and leadership of female civil rights workers. Consider what the overwhelming myth of the Sit-in phenomenon would look like had a White woman put herself in harm's way first instead of four Black men and later the Black coed I described? What a feeding frenzy of the press would have followed. The psychology of the archetypal fragile White maiden daring to engage in civil disobedience might well have become the dominant myth of Greensboro rather than the young men. Symbols and their power reflect our own psychology. The young Black women, whether from Bennett or A&T were never treated by the press or even the dominant scholarly studies as fragile young women that needed protection. They were simply ignored. Consider why there are so many more media photos of Bennett's White student than of Bennett's majority Black women?

A&T State University and its graduates and Greensboro citizens are not alone in their sins of omission. This chapter will examine why the coed described and her schoolmates faded behind a curtain of near invisibility and failed to capture the popular imagination of the city of Greensboro as it told itself its proud story. Mention of Bennett College in the Greensboro International Civil Rights Museum is limited to a few brief sentences. Willa Player is not pictured in the museum. It is important to note that the changing times have brought a few important breakthroughs in this oversight, and that feminist scholarship has had a lot to do with that. As noted, a few scholars have themselves engaged in in-depth research and more have called for an increase in such studies. This book is in part a response to that call. As Martin Luther King once said, "We are here to make the invisible visible".

The United Methodist Church was one of the major financial supporters of Bennett College during the 60s. The college is still an affiliated institution with a major relationship to the church. Methodism had its own struggle with responding to the Christian mandate of brotherhood and equality. The Central Jurisdiction of the United Methodist Church was effectively a way of segregating the church. To further understand the reasons for the invisibility of Bennett we need to be aware of the role of the church in securing that history. It is a microcosm of the divided mind of America on matters of race.

When one considers the support the church gave the College and the activities of President Player and the students, the Methodist church comes out on the right side of history. Bennett drew considerable financial support from the Methodist connection. The church provided a safe space for the activism and participation of the students, faculty and administration. Of course Player was in the difficult position of answering to the church while at the same time expressing her unwavering support of the students. We can only surmise that this was successfully finessed by her, as there was no withdrawal of support. On the other hand, the church was significantly silent on the prophetic role being played by the college and their president. There was no national recognition of this as late as 1996.

Barbara Isaacs gives an astute and well crafted assessment of this omission in her dissertation, *The Lunch Counter Struggle, 1960-1963: Women Remapping the Boundaries of Race, Gender and Vocation*. Isaacs gives several examples of this silencing of important activities of Bennett. Among them, a book by Alice G. Knott, *Fellowship of Love: Methodist Women Changing American Racial Attitudes*, published in 1996 by Abington Press, a Methodist press. Knott never mentions Player or her courageous stand during the Greensboro movement, but instead chooses to identify the role of Susie Jones, wife of David D. Jones, Player's predecessor, in the church's attempt to respond nationally to the racial struggle. Mrs. Jones' activities were not directly related to the lunch counter or Greensboro movement (Isaacs, 72).

Grant S. Schokley, in *Heritage and Hope, The African American Presence in United Methodism*, summarizes Willa Player's presidency as follows: "During her administration at Bennett College, it became one of the first senior Negro colleges admitted to membership in the Southern Association of Colleges and schools" (qtd. in Isaacs, 70). He had noted Methodists who played major roles during 1940-1968, with no mention of Player's work in successfully heading a Methodist college during the tumultuous years of the 60s movement, probably the most difficult challenge in her entire career at Bennett.

In her thoughtful and honest work, Isaacs proclaims: "An essential step in the repentance of the Methodist church is to make historically viable the contribution of Willa Player and students of Bennett College...who contributed to the changing of American racial attitudes in the early 1960s" (75). Also covered by Isaacs is the reaction of the Methodist church in Lynchburg Virginia to two White women who sat in, in Lynchburg. They were students from Randolph Macon for Women. We will briefly review this so that we might compare the two Methodist institutions. It is Isaacs' conclusion that the contradictory state of the Methodist church regarding race relations contributed to the "invisibility" (a word also used by Isaacs) of the Bennett students and Willa Player.

In the 1950s, the Methodist church was silent regarding the racial integration of Southern campuses. "The Methodist church would not acknowledge the essential role of Bennett women in igniting the modern Civil Rights Movement. It would not take a courageous stand against the South's Jim Crow laws. It remained silent" (Isaacs, 198). Meanwhile the local Methodist Ministers Fellowship of the Greensboro area wrote a letter to Player in support of the Sit-ins on February 16, 1960 signed by Dr. Leon Stubbs (Player papers).

It must be noted that the church's support of the college by not withdrawing funds or pressuring its president to make students stop the demonstrating was a major factor in the continuing success of the Bennett participation. But it was an indication of the split personality of the United Methodist stance during those days of change. Also a curiously contradictory fact was the passionate writing of *motive* magazine, which appealed to Methodist students all over the country to respond to the call for racial justice. This magazine was the official publication of the

Methodist Student Movement and underwritten by the United Methodist Church.

On Dec 14, 1960, Mary Edith Bentley and Rebecca Mays Owen, the White students from Randolph-Macon Woman's College, were arrested for sitting in at a drugstore counter in Lynchburg Virginia, in sympathy and solidarity with the Black student movement. (For a complete discussion of this case see the Barbara Isaacs dissertation.) Their experience sheds light on the Bennett experience because Randolph-Macon Woman's College is a liberal arts Methodist college located in the South. As a White institution it furnishes us with a revealing comparison in our discussion of the invisibility of women activists. The young women of Randolph-Macon Woman's College were to face the severe criticism of their president, the Methodist churches, and other denominations there in Lynchburg, the shunning of their classmates and the citizens of Lynchburg. They were presented to the whole student body as arrogant, incompetent, and were not allowed to engage in a discussion with their president, Dr. William F. Quillian, said to be a devout Methodist. To keep their witness discredited and invisible they were shamed in front of the other students. They were tried in court and served 20 of their 30 days rather than pay bail, which was their choice.

As Isaacs noted, "they had broken no civil law, but cultural mandates of proper female decorum and propriety," or I would say, "respectability" as defined by their culture. Isaacs goes on to say: "In the eyes of Randolph-Macon Woman's College and the Virginia Conference of the Methodist Church, Owen and Bentley had trespassed on the Southern code of Honor; they trespassed on this code…They brought humiliation to the community" (156).

Randolph-Macon Woman's College was steeped in the Southern way of being properly female. Mary Bentley was shunned by her church and not allowed to play her senior recital there. She was the daughter of a Methodist minister.

Nationally there was support for their "courageous witness," but area Methodists refused a vote of praise for the same courageous and deep convictions noted nationally by the church. The Lynchburg District Methodist Conference took no action of support for the two women. They wanted them to be invisible. One of their members said, "The less we say about this the better off we'll be" (qtd, Isaacs, 176). The comparison of Randolph-Macon and Bennett points graphically to the racial divide of this American history. While Bennett was born out of the need to educate newly emancipated slaves, Randolph-Macon College was part of the Southern traditional way of life that had enslaved these same people. They revealed their origins in their reaction to the stand taken by students. The reaction of both sets of Methodists involved reveals the degree of investment in local customs and mores. The segment of the Methodist Church that supported Bennett financially and on the Bennett board, by and large did not live in Greensboro or in North Carolina. The Lynchburg area Methodists supported their class/cultural origins in the matter, not the Christian witness of their students. Those who step outside the official sanctioned story of the culture are often rejected because those who seek to control the story have a vested interest in telling it their way. That was not the story they wanted told about the cultured and civilized Methodist school and its students in Lynchburg.

In the Lynchburg District Methodist Conference, a segment of their 1960 resolution supported the establishment and work of the biracial committee appointed by the City Council to bring about racial understanding. That part of the resolution was approved (Isaacs, 176). Apparently it was much more threatening to them that these young women had taken it upon themselves to change the story of Lynchburg their way. They had wrested control of social change away from the establishment of the city council (no doubt mostly if not all White males in 1960). This was not to be allowed.

In contrast to Quillian, Player's unwavering support of her students is a frequently related story among Bennett graduates and those in Greensboro who are most familiar with the Greensboro movement.

Through inviting public figures that would give their considerable influence to the movement (Thurgood Marshall, and Benjamin Mays to name two), Player continued to insist that the students were doing the right thing. She never insisted that they leave jail even after they were offered release. They were staying as a point of honor they had agreed upon. However, her presence and influence in the movement is hardly known outside the Greensboro community. As late as 2007 an article by Gerri Bates in the *Journal of Negro Education*, entitled "These Hallowed Halls, African American Women College and University Presidents" names a woman appointed in 1970 as the first African American woman college president since Mary McLeod Bethune. Player became president of Bennett in 1956 and was president until 1966. Incredibly, she is completely omitted from Bates' list of African American College presidents, a case of total invisibility.

Although Bennett was very well thought of among the community of educators in Player's time, and was well known among the middle class parents looking for private schools for their daughters, we must be aware that Player herself had a reticent and modest personality. Her quiet restraint was a hallmark of the way she carried herself. Her reluctance to allow *Mademoiselle Magazine* to come to the campus for a feature story came partly from her fear that Bennett's way of life would be misunderstood by the popular media. They did come to the campus in 1965 and Player was not happy with the results. After the publication of the story she expressed her regret that she had given permission. [3] In an age that was just beginning to explore the power of information in the media, she was not comfortable

---

[3] Player confided this in person to the writer.

with exposure over which she had no control. Also her deep sense of responsibility to the parents and their daughters gave her pause as the students stepped out into history with all the risks that entailed. She was careful to alert the parents and explain to them her position and the position of the College regarding the activism; she had been meticulous through the years to inform parents of campus policy. Her reluctance for Bennett Women to take the lead in the Sit-in action without the presence of A&T men had everything to do with protecting these women. Player was a daughter of the South. She had been born in, and spent her childhood in Mississippi. She knew the wrath of racists and what could happen and before it was all over she would experience strong pressure from the Greensboro establishment to call her "girls" back to campus.

Generally, she kept her cards close to her chest in all things that would expose the college or its students in threatening or negative ways. As Darlene Clark Hine said; "Because of the interplay of racial animosity, class tensions, gender role differentiation, and regional economic variations, Black women as a rule developed a politics of silence and adhered to a cult of secrecy, a culture of dissemblance to protect the sanctity of the inner aspects of their lives" (qtd. in Isaacs, 103).

I am suggesting that the reticence of Player may have added to the complex level of reasons for the habit of putting Bennett's contributions in the background, because publicity writ large was becoming the way to get your story told in the years following the movement. Player would have never been insistent about demanding recognition. It was not her way. What was done was done for the common good. Christian witness was her way and the source of her strong stand on principle. Getting the credit was not the point. That it was done was enough.

Player's convictions about civil rights were tied to her Christian convictions and the 1958 speech to the Fifth Assembly is very strong evidence for this connection (see Chapter One). She continues to make the linkages between civil rights, educational purpose, and Christian belief system in a 1962 article "Basic Values in American Education," published in the *World Outlook*, a Methodist publication, in February. In this article the lineage of historically Black Colleges is reviewed as she makes a case for the logic of the leadership of Black colleges in the struggle for equality and racial justice. If we had any doubts about why a Black Methodist College would be in the forefront of the struggle she lays that to rest. Her natural reticence to be in the spotlight and "take credit" was one thing. Her strong belief that what a Christian college should be doing included witnessing for justice was another.

In this 1962 article we remember what struggles were taking place in Greensboro when Player says that the nation needs as never before the talents of *all* its people. She uses the same inscription on the Bennett bell that opens this book to explain the origins of the College, and next reviews the founding in 1873 by the Freedmen's Aid Society:

> It needed therefore no revision to relate to the changing social scene as it first emerged in 1954 from the decision of the Supreme Court....When the schools and colleges opened in September 1961, we were reminded again that the transition to integration is yet both slow and painful. The Negro College has to play its own particular role for many years. Even should America progress to its highest goal and transition so [that] integration comes to an end, the Negro colleges will take their rightful place among institutions of higher learning serving American youth without regard to race (Player, "Basic Values").

She goes on to say that these colleges are, more than any, prepared to meet the challenges of integration because they have always been open to all.

The subtle and sometimes not so subtle silencing of women during the Civil Rights Movement is now well known. We must be aware that naming and defining the story means challenging the accepted version of the story. In the case of the history we are examining it means challenging patriarchal, racial and even class privilege. It is crucial to ask, what forbidden boundaries did women cross who sat in and marched? After 1965 it is well documented that SNCC became more patriarchal and authoritarian. Paula Giddings records that women were told to "step back" and were accused of wanting to rob black men of their manhood. As we move through the sixties, the Civil Rights Movement goes through the metamorphosis of Black Power and the style of militancy becomes overtly macho. These changes in the movement infect the Black response to methods of social change, duly noted by scholars Giddings, Robnett and others.

More than fifty years have gone by since the 1960 Sit-ins. One must ask the question, how much of the civil rights contribution of women has been submerged into the machismo style of the late 60s and 70s? This way of being infected hip-hop culture. This way of thinking is the legacy of the fear of the loss of Black masculinity and the White attempt to suppress the same. The movement in Greensboro was never about Black power but was about equal rights and access. As women of Bennett we did not think about having to validate our role later in history. It is only as the years went on that we realized we were less and less a part of the official story. The same impulse to tell our story has surfaced nationally with our activist sisters as the scholarship and reporting of what is now history is beginning to be assessed.

According to Stephen F. Lawson, in 1991 the documentary *Eyes on the Prize* failed to include in its narration an analysis of the sexual politics of the racial struggle. He goes on to call for research on women participants in order for there to be a definitive analysis of gender relations. "We need systematic studies of how ordinary women in their role as mothers, wives, workers, church goers, and professionals [and I might add students] affected the nature of the movement" (468). In the study first published by Miles Wolff in 1970, *Lunch at the 5&10*, he mentions the boycott and protest of the local movie theaters in Greensboro in 1937, but incorrectly says that A&T had boycotted the theaters, instead of Bennett where it was conceived and led by the president's daughter. He notes twice that there were White students demonstrating in 1960; we are never told how many Bennett students were present except for the two White Bennett students.

Speaking of the Greensboro Sit-ins, Martin Oppenheimer, in a major work, *The Southern Student Movement: Year 1*, notes: "After the first day they came back with other students, some from other Greensboro colleges. A campus group, the Student Executive Committee for Justice, was organized" (398). Omitting the names of the "other colleges," he lumps Bennett in with two White colleges that were represented by no more than five students all told. Bennett was obviously not understood as having been central to the events, even though the student Executive Committee was co-chaired by Gloria Brown, Bennett president of the student body.

Deidre Flowers explains that earlier researchers had made no mention of the percentage of Bennett College students that were imprisoned, the proportion of Bennett's students arrested, or their level of participation and planning of activities (Flowers, 56).

The late Dr. Dorothy Height, who has been called the founding matriarch of the Civil Rights Movement, and was president of the National Council of Negro Women for over 40 years, reported to Dr. Johnnetta Cole that she was always "bothered that there was not equal concern about women and gender as there was about race" [in the ranks of the movement]. She remarked: "While leadership was male, the backbone of the Civil Rights Movement was most certainly women and youth." Dr. Height shared the story of how the male leadership of the 1963 March on Washington did not allow one Black woman to make one of the major speeches at the March on Washington in 1963. The men objected to having the women seated on the dais. After much arguing and petitioning, Dr. Height was seated off to the side but not on the dais. Some women leaders were introduced, but none was invited to the White House to meet with President Kennedy following the march. Dr. Height gives the impression that she did not want to fight with the men publicly, but preferred an appearance of unity (Cole 86-88).

In Dr. Pauli Murray's essay, *"The Negro Woman in the Quest for Equality,"* she writes about "the tendency to assign women to a secondary ornamental or honoree role instead of partnership role they have earned by their courage, intelligence and dedication":

> I have been increasingly perturbed over the blatant disparity between the major role which Negro women have played and are playing at the crucial grass roots levels of our struggle and the major role of leadership they have been assigned in the national policy making decisions. It is indefensible to call a National March on Washington and send out a call which contains the name of not one single women leader (Murray qtd. in Cole, 88).

It is critical to understand what interaction of gender, politics, and conditioning came together to produce what Isaacs calls the "disremembering" of the Bennett College women who sat at the lunch counters and took a risk that was potentially life threatening. These young women were often blissfully ignorant of what could have happened to them had they perhaps been in a different community. We remember that Fannie Lou Hamer and others like her paid dearly for their threat to White/male/class power. The Bennett women were challenging the conception of reality held by this power. The place of women in the world (Black women especially) was redefined by them in public, and threatened the very cosmic order men had heretofore believed in. This was dangerous business.

In summary I would have to say that the "invisibility" of the Bennett College contribution to the Civil Rights Movement is in some small measure the result of President Player's own tendency toward self effacing behavior and modesty and partly the customary and self-protective dissembling of Black women, but mainly it is due to the cultural silencing of powerful women who chose to act outside the norms set by patriarchy and made themselves visible.

CHAPTER 4

ANOTHER CULTURE

"We are going to have rioting.
We are going to have people killed."
Edward Zane

As I walked to my classes under the walkway leading from one building to the next there was a rainfall of eggs coming from the classroom building. Most of them landed on me. But I wiped my face, looked in disgust at my new dress and walked on to class. Some of the students jeered and called out 'nigger'....Some students yelled, 'You know we don't want you here. Go back to your own school. This is our school!' There was a strange call from a man who identified himself as the Grand Wizard of the Klan. He said, 'You are helping to destroy all that is sacred to the Southern way of life. If you go to Senior High you will live to regret it.' All I could think of as I listened to him condemn me to hell was I wanted to smother him. This ongoing harassment was joined by others who identified themselves as members of the White Citizens Council; they talked mostly about how 'the good Lord did not intend for Blacks to go to school with Whites'. My brothers told me later that members of the Klan and other groups threw things down our chimney. We were lucky that nothing exploded when it landed in the fireplace...White men would come by and cut up or puncture the tires to our car

*and truck. Many of our animals were killed and we
mourned the death of beloved dog. A tree was cut down
across our driveway making it impossible for us to get out
until my brothers cut it up into logs.*

*Our calls to the police were in vain. They did not provide
any significant protection and said 'There is nothing we
can do to prevent these disasters from happening...'
Students would regularly throw rocks at our car...I found
tacks in my seats in the classrooms....The incident that
hurt the worst was the loss of my father's snack bar....It
inexplicably burned down. That was the only time that I
saw my father cry. He just said 'Why this, why this?'...I
wanted to know what it was about being black that made it
necessary to have separate restrooms and water fountains
for us in Woolworth and other downtown stores. (Pfaff,
Boyd interview, 55-58).*

This is not the voice of a Sit-in participant but of a young girl
who took her stand before the 1960 movement. This is the voice
of Josephine Boyd (Bradley) who was the first Black student to
attend Greensboro Senior High. She (and her parents) took the
bold step of desegregating the oldest high school in Greensboro
in 1957. Josephine was only 17 and was entirely alone in her
radical action. We begin to see very clearly through her story
what kind of atmosphere existed in the city of Greensboro and
what the Bennett women walked into when they walked out of
their dorms toward downtown Greensboro, Woolworth, and
history. How dangerous was it to defy the cultural norms of
Greensboro, North Carolina in 1960? More to the point, how
dangerous was it for women to defy the normative behavior of
both race and gender?

We began the book by saying that the appearance of Bennett
College could be misleading. This distinction between appearance and reality is also true of the city of Greensboro, its White
citizens and its Black citizens in different ways. In 1960 the

students who participated walked into a culture other than the "official" culture of Greensboro.

The reactions recorded in many interviews reveal that the Sit-ins of 1960 became an awakening for the White citizens. Newspaper accounts teach us that they expressed surprise and outrage, depending on their orientation. If we can believe their words, the men running the city, the businessmen, and the power structure were caught without the awareness that the Black citizens of Greensboro had for years been frustrated and dissatisfied.

James Townsend, then city manager, said: "I think that the reason the students picked Greensboro was due to the fact that race relations in Greensboro had always been good, but we were mistaken" (Pfaff, Townsend interview, 101).

It appears that the Sit-ins brought Townsend to the realization that race relations were not good in his town. He seems not to understand that while sitting in in Greensboro may have made sense to the adults involved, Greensboro was simply the place where these particular young people found themselves at the time. Of course, quasi spontaneous action of this kind is also only possible when the motivation for the action has been building for some time. In this case African American frustration was hundreds of years old. The real nature of the African American mind set was hidden in plain view, as it were, partly because of deliberate dissembling which Black people had been practicing for three hundred years, and partly because of the deliberate blindness of Whites.

The official assessment of the climate of the city (that usually quoted by city "fathers") was that Greensboro was the "most liberal Southern city". Chafe gives us an astute analysis of the attitudes of White leaders in Greensboro in his book *Civilities and Civil Rights*. He explains how the progressive mystique of Greensboro was that it valued civility over honesty. Arnold Schiffman, businessman, appeared to be overly worried that "Black people cannot enjoy the privilege [of eating at

Woolworth] until they earn it by their behavior" (Pfaff,
Schiffman interview, 112). He goes on to say, "We did not try to
define a level of behavior, appearance, or cleanliness," revealing
an attitude that could only be called paternalistic at best and
racist at worst.

The image of Greensboro and of North Carolina that was
commonly held was that this was an area more "progressive"
than much of the South. The only problem was that the
underbelly of Greensboro contained the antipathy of many
Whites, either mild or extreme. At the very least their paternalistic White privileged attitudes had prevented them from
seeing that people denied equal access to the advantages of
citizenship will at some point call for a reckoning. "What
happens to a dream deferred?" asked poet Langston Hughes,
"Does it sag like a heavy load or does it explode?"

Chafe writes, "Civility was what White progressivism was
all about, a way of dealing with people and problems that made
good manners more important that substantial action" (Chafe, 8).
This is why George Simkins, Black dentist and activist who had
fought to integrate the golf course, said:

> Greensboro is a very, very conservative city. (Civil Rights
> Greensboro library.uncg.edu)   And later he says:
> Greensboro is a very strange city in that Blacks have to
> fight for everything that they get here. I mean they don't
> give one inch. And you have to picket, demonstrate, take
> them to court to get anything done. Other cities around
> Greensboro - Durham, Raleigh, Winston-Salem, and High
> Point – opening up their recreational facilities to people of
> color, whereas Greensboro was closing down everything.
> They would knock us down and we'd get back up and
> continue to fight" (Pfaff, Simkins interview, 12, 13).

That is why Willa Player could say, "I think it was erroneous
to think of Greensboro as a liberal city. It did just enough to
appear to the outside world to be less segregated than other
cities" (Pfaff, Player interview, 21).

One observation that we can safely make is that there was the intense desire to preserve the reputation of the city of Greensboro. The city manager at the time, James Townsend says: "We were determined we wouldn't get Greensboro into the headlines by having a riot where somebody was injured" (Pfaff, Townsend interview 101). George Roach, Greensboro mayor in 1960 says: "I had several requests for an interview on television but I declined; I was concerned about the national image of Greensboro. I wanted it to remain a local incident" (Pfaff, Roach interview, 99).

It should come as no surprise that the city leaders would be concerned about image since image is about money and business coming into the city. On the other hand, the stubbornness of the five and dime restaurant owners was about money and their fear that whites would not patronize downtown businesses if Blacks could eat at their restaurants.

Until 1960, the culture of White Greensboro had consisted of fostering civility within a system of second-class citizenship as long as Black people went quietly about their business and did not ruffle the waters of White privilege.

At the same time that the White leaders of Greensboro wanted to see it as a "liberal community," they appeared to have been terrified at the prospect that a disruption of the status quo would cause chaos and bloodshed in the same city that was supposed to be so liberal, or to put it another way, the story they wanted to tell about themselves was that their city was "nice" at the same time that it maintained White supremacy. Chancellor Blackwell of Woman's College (now UNC-G) in his speech to the student body takes the WC women who had joined in the Sit-ins to task: he mentions "concern for the dangers of physical violence and destruction of property which had faced the students and institutions involved." Also he expresses concern for the "reputation of Greensboro and North Carolina at a time when forward progress in all areas is a reality." Moreover, he questions the wisdom of students becoming involved in "a situation which if unchecked would surely result in violence and bloodshed" (*Civil Rights Greensboro, archives*). This, in what had been called by Ike English, Burlington Industry's chief engineer, "the most liberal community in the Southeast" (Civil Rights Greensboro, library.uncg.edu).

The chancellor went on to say to his students: "The tensions that have been generated now threaten the good relations that have existed between segments of our population. The good will of substantial elements in the community has been jeopardized to the cause of improving race relations. Participation in this demonstration...definitely resulted in increasing the inflammatory quality of the situation" (Civil Rights Greensboro library.uncg.edu).

In the meantime, Edward Zane of the City Council is telling the mayor and the Council that something should be done about the Sit-ins. He admits the Council wanted segregation to remain. He admonishes them that: "It will not work itself out. We are going to have rioting. We're going to have people killed. We're going to have a lot of bad publicity for the city of Greensboro. There's going to be violence if we don't do something" (Pfaff, Zane interview, 103).

Somewhere in the consciousness of those who wanted to believe in what Chafe called the "mystique" of Greensboro lurked the certainty that it was only skin deep (pun intended). The violent shadow of racism was always skulking in the background. Dr. Warren Ashby was a professor at Woman's College. He was frank about this opinion in a 1981 interview and admits that, "The White power structure and business community refused to acknowledge the real demands of the Black community."

"Very early, it was pointed out to me by Black members [of a faculty fellowship group] that they viewed Greensboro as a 'nice nasty' town and when they would say 'nasty' any White person would know that it was a lot 'nastier' than it was 'nice' for them "(Pfaff. Ashby interview, 35). During the 60s Ashby was a professor of Philosophy who tried to foster dialogue between the races in various ways. He had been close to Bennett through Dr. David D. Jones and had spoken on campus.

Meanwhile, on the other side of town, the other culture is having its own experience of Greensboro. Although it has been noted the United Methodist Church, national and Northern did not pressure Willa Player to stop the students' movement, there was resistance from many of the members of the West Market Street United Methodist Church to prevent their minister from welcoming Black Methodists to their church in Greensboro. Once or twice small groups of two or three Black Methodists had attended. The Rev. Dr. Bowles received nasty letters and there were people who threatened to bar the doors of their churches in town if Blacks tried to attend. Dr. Bowles was preaching integration from the pulpit of West Market Street United Methodist Church (*Civil Rights Greensboro, interview of Ike English*).

Much more intense than a few people threatening to bar the doors of their churches was the life Black citizens of Greensboro experienced in the mid fifties which prepared the ground for the Sit-ins. The golf course case, which Dr. George Simkins of the NAACP led to establish the right of Blacks to use the city-owned golf course, and the other efforts of the NAACP to desegregate public facilities — swimming pools, tennis courts, Cone hospital, and the schools — these efforts were hard fought and extremely unwelcome in the city. The cross burning that took place on the lawn of Bennett professor, Dr. Edward Edmonds (actually part of the Bennett College campus) was an indication of this attitude.

Dr. King's visit, then, was a culmination of many activities that should have indicated the reality of Greensboro's true colors. The Sit-ins occurred against the backdrop of foot dragging and deliberate defiance of the 1954 Supreme Court ruling on school desegregation in Greensboro. The culture of "niceness" in Greensboro did not extend to embracing the integration of the Greensboro school system. Uppermost in the minds of Greensboro's African American citizens had to be the experience of Josephine Boyd, the first Black student at Greensboro Senior High School in her senior year, 1957-58. As we have seen, Josephine as a lone Black female student, had to deal with overt hatred and resentment, including threats from the Klan, the White Citizens Council, egg throwing and ugly verbal attacks throughout the year. These threats extended to her family and her principal as well.

Once the Sit-in movement began, the Black community experienced fully a Greensboro that they always knew was there, from civilized and dignified exclusion to the edge of violence barely averted. The climate into which the Bennett women marched was full of racially negative messages and was overtly threatening. For example, according to Chafe, the downtown YWCA "was dominated by middle and upper class White women....The YWCA had held interracial meetings during the 1940s but it was always under circumstances that ensured compliance with the traditional racial etiquette." The YWCA of Bennett and A&T were invited to citywide meetings downtown but not at a time when a meal would be served [to avoid the taboo of eating together], (Chafe, 40, 41).

When the first African American sat down at the lunch counter the appearance of deference to Whites had been fully broken in public. No one could pretend any longer that the civilized meetings of the YWCA just happened not to be at a mealtime. No one could hide the fact that the taboo of eating together existed, or that it was really about second-class citizenship and enforcing the Southern caste system. With the participation of Bennett women, the genteel Southern women had come face to face with the reality that they considered the genteel Southern African American women inferior and unfit to eat with them.

Jo Spivey was the reporter from the *Greensboro Record* who covered the Sit-ins. Her concern that "some of these picketing students, particularly the girls from Bennett might get hurt," was expressed to General James R. Townsend who promised that there would be protection. (Pfaff), Spivey interview, 71).

William Jackson from the Greensboro police says that by the end of the first week, "It was beginning to get a little nasty....In regards to the Klan stuff most of our troubles were with White teenagers....There was a danger of violent eruption to a degree, but not great....I saw a time within the store itself that looked like it was going to be very explosive, but we were able to get those that were kicking up...." (*Civil Rights Greensboro*, William Henry Chafe, Oral History Collection July 12, 1977).

The Students endured heckling from the crowd, starting on the second day. Groups of tough White teenagers were in the store and driving by, yelling obscenities while picketing was going on.

Jo Spivey reports that she was harassed by the Klan for several years for various stories that she reported on. She revealed that they called her house and frightened her young child on the phone, "scared her to death," she said. (Schlosser, interview: www.greensboro Sit-ins).

Ann Dearsley gave a particularly detailed description of the intimidation she was subject to as a White student from Woman's College:

> *There was a large White crowd behind us....Our position suddenly became clear, and the crowd became extremely threatening...It was a very scary three hours sitting in that lunch space because the crowd got closer and closer. There was a man with a knife behind my back....It was obvious to me that the police would not support us and we sat there feeling really very scared and totally unable to move because there were hundreds of people in that very narrow store. We said to each other how do we get out of here at 5:00? There were hundreds of hostile people filling the store and blocking the exits...The store was full of angry people who didn't like what we were doing.*

The A&T football players linked arms around us and walked up those narrow aisles to the sidewalk with us in the middle as members of the crowd taunted us....the guys opened up their flying wedge and put the three of us in a cab. That's how we got back to the campus. To have walked back would have been dangerous. It was an extremely scary time for me. (Pfaff, Dearsley interview, 90-92).

As she covered the events that were unfolding for the *News and Record*, Reporter Jo Spivey described the reactions of Whites who were against the students.

The spectators were more militant than the marchers. Sometimes they were hecklers, sometimes they were passive observers...some of them brought their kids to see it which I couldn't understand. I saw some violence in the store, mostly pushing, jostling by some of the counter demonstrators.

They didn't physically hurt these people but there were some White men, probably KKK members who heckled the Bennett girls studying at the counter saying such things as "Look at that nigger, she thinks she can read."

Sat Feb 6 was a very tense day. A girl got her teeth knocked in from a thrown rock, and some other people were injured. Some people dropped jugs of water off the top of the King Cotton [Hotel] onto the demonstrators as they marched past below (Pfaff, Spivey interview, 128-129).

Long time activist and Sit-in participant Lewis Brandon remembers well the atmosphere that faced the students as they sat in on February 6, 1960. Lewis was a member of the Student Executive Committee for Justice. He says the tactic of harassment was used to arrest two men from A&T. His roommate Donald Lyons was burned when lighted cigarettes were put in his pockets. There were A&T, Bennett, and Dudley High School students there.

Sat morning Feb 6, the Woolworth manager closed the counters. Things were very tense that day. We were in

Kress and I looked up and all I could see were blue and gold football jerseys [A&T colors]. Some White bullies began to move out of the way. The football team had come down and at that time we had some guys weighing as much as 300 pounds. We went up to Woolworth and... there was jostling for position. When they announced the counters were closed, we marched back to campus. As we walked past the King Cotton Hotel people threw bags of water and other things out the windows. (Pfaff, Brandon interview, 113).

Joseph McNeil recalls a stink bomb being thrown on the picketers (www.sitin.com). Jibreel Khazan understood well the ethos of Greensboro that was under the veneer of gentility. "We had nightly threats," he said, "People called and threatened to kill us...They said, 'We will kill you if you niggers go down there'" (www.sitins.com). Before the Sit-ins, the Ashby's, Warren and Helen, had experienced harassment and ugly phone calls simply for having interracial student discussion groups with students from Bennett College and Woman's College in their home.

It is fair to say that the atmosphere in the city included the certainty long held idea in the Black Community of Greensboro that things were grossly unequal and unfair. Dr. David Jones and others of his stature had done what they could to help make changes and call attention to the old ingrained injustices. Dr. Hobart Jarrett of Bennett spoke out about bloc voting by Black citizens. The Rev. Otis Hairston Sr. said that the Greensboro Citizens Association controlled the voting of the Black Community by block voting as the only way to develop power. It was organized in 1959 with Dr. Hobart Jarrett as President (Pfaff, Hairston interview, 20).

In the years preceding the Sit-ins, White friends of the African American community, like Warren Ashby, had made sincere but safe gestures. In the 50s, 12 to 15 people, including people from Bennett and A&T, would meet for bag lunches at the American Friends Service Committee College Program (Pfaff, Ashby interview, 34). Dr. William Hampton was elected to the Greensboro City Council in 1951. Dr. David Jones was elected to the school board in 1954. Some small progress was made. There was an inter-campus faculty group that met for several years involving faculty from A&T and WC; however, according to Franklin Parker (faculty member UNCWC) he was prevented from having a colleague from A&T come to speak at Woman's College by the chancellor who threatened him with the loss of his job (Pfaff, 41).

Life for African Americans was a checkerboard of overt hostility on the one hand, and White people who made tentative gestures of good will on the other, which almost always failed to derail the prevailing deep seated racist culture. Jennie and Franklin Parker's daughter and two other White students made an effort to support Josephine Boyd in 1957 when she was the lone Black student at Greensboro High. As Jennie Parker remembers those days:

> Our daughter Ginger...went to Josephine and told her they would like to eat with her in the lunch room....At least one day I went out and sat with them. Things were thrown, marbles, all sorts of things like that. Our daughter and Julia [one of the other students] receive threatening phone calls saying things like 'How does it feel to be a nigger lover'? And so on...

She describes the Greensboro High students who rallied around Josephine to protect her, noting the harassment and threatening phone calls received by school officials from angry Whites (Pfaff, Jennie Franklin interview, 45).

We know from Jo Spivy's words that little children were not immune to the fear tactics used by those who were against Black equality. Attorney J. Kenneth Lee shared his experience with Pfaff: " As virtually the only Black attorney in town that took civil rights cases, I received anonymous hate calls. One night my wife and I went [next door]. When we returned our six year old son was hysterical. Someone had called and graphically described what they were going to do to his daddy. We had to take him to the emergency room to get him calmed down" (Pfaff, Lee interview, 58).

Of course it is impossible to relate all the instances of either negative or positive experiences in the days preceding the Sit-in action and the subsequent Greensboro movement. But it is clear without any doubt that life in Greensboro was lived within an ever-present shadow of hatred, and furthermore, not lived without severe repercussions for those who dared to go against the prevailing mores. The climate the Bennett women walked into when they walked into Woolworth was unpredictable, certain to be difficult, and undeniably dangerous.

꙰꙰꙰꙰꙰꙰꙰

CHAPTER 5

PATTERNS OF PROGRESS

*"The Greensboro Sit-in may have been to some extent derivative
of the lunch counter Sit-in in Wichita, Kansas in 1958."*
Ronald Walters

While the Greensboro Sit-ins were in some ways unique, it was not the first city to experience this technique for creating social change. Morris Alden in his 1981 study of the Sit-in movement lists 15 cities where Sit-ins took place between 1957 and 1960. CORE was successful with a Sit-in as early as 1942 (Oppenheimer, 396). This said, how typical was the Sit-in and Civil Rights Movement in Greensboro? What useful patterns can we observe? How did Bennett fit into these patterns?

There are ways in which the Greensboro Sit-ins fit into a national pattern that might extend our understanding of our city and its activists. The pre-1960 Sit-ins documented in cities such as Tulsa, Wichita, Oklahoma City and St. Louis (Oppenheimer, 397), reveal that, contrary to a spontaneous decision, there was often some long term planning preceding the actual Sit-ins.

Ronald Walters documents his decision to Sit-in in 1958 in Wichita Kansas in an article entitled "Standing up in America's Heartland," published in *American Visions*. In the spring of 1958, as a young college student, he decided that it was time to do something about segregation of the lunch counter where he had to eat standing up.

> *No flash of insight led me to confront this humiliation. It was like other defining moments in that era of growing political consciousness within the Black community, born of discrete acts of oppression and resistance... However what emerged in popular history as the origins of the movement are the Montgomery Bus Boycott and the "first" Sit-in in Greensboro in 1960....The Greensboro Sit-in may have been to some extent derivative of the lunch counter Sit-in in Wichita Kansas in 1958 (Walters, 20).*

Ten young people began the Wichita Sit-in with Walters on Saturday July 19, 1958. He was concerned for the safety of the two women with them. Reminiscent of Greensboro, two White students joined them from Wichita University. In the fourth week of demonstrations, during which White resistance became more and more dangerous, the lunch counters were opened.

Walters continues, building the case that it was highly unlikely that the Greensboro four did not know about the effort in Wichita:

> *The link between the Midwest actions and the Greensboro Sit-in was more than just sequence. Ezell Blair and Joseph McNeil were officers in the Greensboro NAACP youth council. It is highly unlikely that they were unfamiliar with the Sit-ins elsewhere in the county led by their organizational peers. At the 51st conference of the NAACP held in Philadelphia in 1960 the national officer recognized its local youth councils for the work they were doing in breaking down lunch counter segregation. At that conference, Robert C. Weaver and Roy Wilkins recognized Wichita and Oklahoma City for desegregating lunch counters" (Walters, 23).*

The point is that like other popular accounts of history (such as the Rosa Parks story) we seldom know the complete story, and also that the recounting of Greensboro as the "first" is the result of the popular need to create myth out of highly significant events. Also it is interesting that following Wichita, the NAACP began to support the Sit-in movement, although it had turned down Walters and his group. "We received a telegram," he writes, "from Herbert Wright national NAACP youth secretary, saying that the contemplated Sit-in [in Wichita] was not regarded as an NAACP tactic and that therefore we would not receive the benefit of legal coverage." Later Wright would lead a team of NAACP lawyers providing legal assistance for the wave of Sit-ins on the South that followed.

Many of these Sit-ins in various cities were initiated or partnered with civil rights organizations such as CORE and the NAACP and these efforts received substantial backing from their community leaders, churches, schools, etc. (Morris, 748). In Greensboro the NAACP and CORE were both involved in supporting the movement both in the lunch counter effort and later in the second wave of the movement.

Morris reminds us that there was ongoing communication between NAACP chapters in various parts of the country. He believes it was no accident that the early Sit-ins occurred between 1957 and 1960. When Mrs. Daisy Bates led the Black students into Central High in Little Rock in 1957, they were associated with the NAACP youth council. Chapters of the NAACP were in touch throughout the country.

The "spontaneous" nature of the Sit-ins in Greensboro and elsewhere had the same kind of domino effect as had the young demonstrators of the "Arab Spring." Only the technology was different. The youngsters in Greensboro were not living in a vacuum. They were very aware of events in the larger world. Many of the Bennett women who were motivated to Sit-in and to carry through until 1963 had been active in the NAACP student chapter on the campus whose faculty advisors were members.

Without a doubt, their professors had influenced them. We will hear their voices in a later chapter, as they mention such teachers as The Rev. John Hatchett, Dr. Edward Edmonds, and Dr. Hobart Jarrett and others. As Morris explains, students and seasoned activists were anchored to the same organizations. Funds for jail bonds, boycotts, etc, were tactics familiar to community leaders (Morris, 764).

Pulling together the fragments of the Bennett civil rights story, one becomes aware that it is an institutional story. That is, that no one individual inspired, acted alone, or accomplished anything alone. This college would never have had the central role its members played without the participation of its adult members, its administration and its students being of like mind. The support of the faculty staff, administration, and the actual activist participation of faculty members, — when the movement became a community movement — must be included to make the story complete. Their support of the women students and their participation was critical and necessary, for the boldness of the Bennett women was partially due to the feeling that there were adults standing behind, and with them.

We have noted the strong presence of Dr. Willa Player in this scenario. It was an institutional scenario that was carried through until its resolution in 1964. No one could say officially that the college was doing this, but the college *was* doing it in its solidarity with the students and with the community. So as we look at the Bennett women we must note the courageous and significant influence of the Bennett faculty (women and men) who were in the background and forefront of the events as well.

As events moved from a focus on the lunch counters to a broader context of public accommodations in general, the collaboration of students and civil rights organizations became central to the success of the movement.

It was not an accident that the lunch counter activism spread almost immediately from Woolworth to S.H. Kress's and then beyond. It was the inevitable conclusion that any thinking person would draw — it was the system of segregation that had to be deconstructed, not one store's practices.

So the patterns we see include the four young men initially "sitting down" with the consciousness that these things or things like this had occurred in other parts of the country. They had conversations that we can date from the winter of 1959 with John Hatchett, and Bennett students, and with Ralph Johns, a merchant in Greensboro who tried to inspire them to make a move. At least two of them were NAACP members, and they had teachers and parents who inspired them. At any rate the ground had been "prepared" in a number of ways. The proliferation of the Sit-ins to other students in other locations and states is a documented story and unique in its rapidity, scope, and connection to the Greensboro influence. The fire caught in Greensboro, died back to embers, and blazed up again in the fall of 1961 to take the city by storm and change the racial dynamic there forever.

The role of Bennett women reflects significant patterns in the national story. Speaking of the participation of women in the Civil Rights Movement, Charles Payne, who studied the activism of Black women in the Mississippi Delta, notes: "We know beyond dispute the women were frequently the dominant force in the movement. *Their historical invisibility is perhaps the most compelling example of the way our shared images of the movement distort and confuse the historical reality*" (my italics) (qtd. in Isaacs, 470).

The emphasis that has been given to the presence of White women in Greensboro in various accounts by scholars and reporters is striking. The cultural taboo represented by White women demonstrating with Black men would have had shock value to White writers and readers. Wolff, in *Lunch at the 5 & 10,* gives major attention and space to the White students and their colleges (46).

As we look at patterns of participation by women in the national struggle for civil rights, it must be said that A&T women were also very important to these efforts. Bennett women were not the lone representatives of their sex. However, that is a story that must be told by A&T just as the history of the participation of White women in the movement is a story in itself. These individual accounts matter because the dynamic of race and gender is a major part of how the struggle for liberation has been played out in America. The history of women activists in America is vast and complicated.

If we just list some very brief examples of women's activism, and the risks women have taken and compare this to the Greensboro events, we might discover some revealing repeated motifs that further clarify the Greensboro experience. These examples are only the tip of the huge iceberg of contributions women have made to civil rights progress in America. They are only meant to serve as illustrative of the gender dynamics that had been going on for years in the struggle for liberation, and the forces that also affected Bennett women.

As early as 1949, over 700 workers, a majority of them Black women, voted to strike when Memphis Furniture refused to sign a contract with local 282 (Green, 186), a rather remarkable move considering the deep and dangerous racism characteristic of the area. Also in 1949 in Montgomery, Alabama, African American women organized the Women's Political Council. This council communicated strategy and tactics essential for mass mobilization. In April of 1955 five Black women employees objected to the presence of an elderly Black woman employee dressed as a "mammy" at a restaurant. She was wearing a bandana around her head and ringing a bell stationed outside the Patio 6 restaurant. The women who objected were arrested, jailed, charged with disorderly conduct, found guilty, and fined in city court (Green, 183).

In another example of Black women's activism, during the Garbage workers strike in Memphis, the NAACP women's division increased to 500 very rapidly indicating the extent to which women had already established important networks through civic clubs, women's organizations and churches despite their lack of representation on the NAACP Board (Green, 198).

"Civic club activism linked concerns about home, family, schools and community to collective political action and involved large numbers of women" (Green p. 200). In the Memphis Garbage Workers strike women embraced activism for racial and economic justice...Rather than aspiring to an ideal of womanhood in which they relinquished their roles as activists and wage earner to male heads of household they presented themselves as equals in both roles (Green, 253). Historically women have seen the connection between improving the quality of life for their children and families and improving educational opportunities and political activity.

Charles Payne looked closely at the movement in Greenwood, Mississippi, and concluded that the men led but the women organized. What he said was: "While formal leadership positions in movement organization remained overwhelmingly a male preserve, the growth and sustenance of the movement relied upon the activities of its female participants" (qtd. Ling, "A Question of Leadership," 290). Belinda Robnett explains that organizing is leading and cautions that it is important to understand the various functions of leadership, as does Bernice McNair Bennett, who studied Black women in the Civil Rights Movement in her work, *Invisible Southern Black Women Leaders in the Civil Rights Movement*. Although this is only a quick glimpse into what is a major, even epic tale of the courageous power of women in the history of human rights, these and other interpretations of the role of women give us a context in which to put Bennett women and their involvement in this great movement for human justice.

Payne's interpretation can be said to reflect Greensboro to a certain extent. Bennett women played a dominant role in the sustaining presence of the Greensboro movement. As Lewis Brandon, participate and A&T graduate said to this writer, "Without those Bennett women, we would not have been able to sustain the efforts in the summer [of 1960] and on to the victories of 1964."

To quote Robnett, "The success of a social movement is an intermediate layer of leadership whose task includes bridging potential constituents and adherents as well as potential formal leaders to the movement" (qtd. Ling, "A Question of Leadership." 289). Robnett coined the term "bridge leaders" to indicate women who bridged the gap between the masses of people and formal leadership. You could also say that interpretation, recruitment and building connections in the community constitutes an enormous amount of work which women often did without the high visibility accorded the "leaders."

During the Montgomery Bus Boycott, bridge leadership via the Women's Political Council helped victims of White economic reprisals, and recruited participants one to one that kept the movement afloat. The energy that galvanizes social action is very difficult to sustain over long periods of time. Many of Greensboro's White leaders expressed the opinion that the lunch counter and its following movement would "burn itself out and blow over." It is easy to understand this assumption. The hard work of social change requires willingness to take a considerable risk, a long-term commitment and an ability to defer the gratification of success. People fall by the wayside; volunteers must be found to sustain the vision.

According to Ling, SNCC relied on bridge leaders, lay women, such as beauticians, domestics, and grass roots women to sustain itself while conventional gender attitudes were strong and a core of males remained in the titled positions of power ("A Question of Leadership," 293).

Hobart Jarrett reported in his interview with William Chafe that the negotiations with Greensboro Kress manager and other White leaders, and the Greensboro Citizens Association (Black citizens), included no women. "In that day nobody was pushing the women's cause" (Chafe, Jarrett interview, *Civil Rights Greensboro*). While Jarrett's perspective is clearly accurate on the surface, one could say that by placing themselves squarely in the center of history the women of Bennett were pushing the "women's cause" without having to say a word about it.

The struggle engaged in by Ella Baker and other women at SCLC on the national level is well documented and has been noted in this work. Ella Baker, in describing her departure from SCLC in disgust, saw the basic problem as her gender, compounded by the preponderance of male ministers whose culture put women in a second-class position. Ms. Septima Clark, another veteran activist who came to work at SCLC in 1961, also found it to be a man's domain. She said in an interview: "Those men didn't have any faith in women, none whatsoever. They just thought that women were sex symbols and had no contribution to make" (Ling, *Gender and the Civil Rights Movement*, 106).

What happened to the story of Bennett College's role in the Greensboro movement is part of a national pattern. This writer is still meeting people today who look surprised when told that more than 200 Bennett women went to jail in the movement of 1962-64 in Greensboro. A retired professor from UNC-G said, "Oh, I had no idea!" when this writer asked her. She said, "I thought it was about A&T".

Finally, a look at the national patterns reveals significant parallels with the Greensboro movement. First, the students' role in the activism was supported, partly inspired by, and certainly collaborated with by adult led organizations, a pattern we see all over the country, particularly after the initial action. In the case of Bennett, it was an institutional effort, participated in by a wide range of college constituents, although the number of faculty members may have been limited, their influence was significant.

We know that the NAACP of Greensboro and the Citizen's Association were led by adults and that later in the movement many of the churches and their ministers supported the movement.

Secondly, Bennett women were on the cutting edge of the movement and given credit by some participants for sustaining activities with their consistent presence and numbers, although the visible leadership remained male with the exception of Willa Player, who is consistently mentioned in interviews, local accounts and some post civil rights era scholarly works, even though she was not included in the Greensboro Citizens Association, and there is little mention of her in the International Civil Rights Museum of Greensboro.

Finally the developing ethos within the national movement excluded women as major players in the official narrative. Similarly, the subsequent and lingering perception in the popular narrative of Greensboro relegates Bennett Women to minor players in the historical narrative, so that many of the city's citizens are unaware of the actual role of the college and its students.

The term "womanism" fits well the role of Bennett women in the Greensboro movement as it does with all bridge leaders around the country, because the need to overcome oppression for all people trumped the need to be an imitation of the traditional "gentility " of Southern womanhood and also the need to be seen as the equal of men. There is no indication that Bennett women were resentful of their role in the movement. They felt themselves to be powerful and assertive in their own right and did not see the "Bennett ideal" (a model of cultured and ladylike behavior that they were inspired to emulate) as contradictory to their participation in the movement. Stepping out into leadership roles, having non-traditional careers was part of the Bennett ideal after all.

While Wolff in his work *Lunch at the 5 & 10*, does not mention Bennett women specifically, he tantalizes us with his description of the Greensboro movement: "But it was the girls who supplied the fervor and in many cases kept the movement going where it had slowed down. When picketing started, it was the girls who were the most faithful about going on the line every day" (Wolff, 158). One wishes he had been gone further and reported which college those girls came from. As in many accounts the men are identified as being from A&T (which of course they were), but all the girls were just "the girls" lumped together and unless they were White, not identified by institution. There is room for some confusion here, since we know with certainty that at least two of the Bennett women were White, and one of the Woman's College students who participated was Black. We can assume with educated certainty that a large number of these "girls" were Bennett women, a fact corroborated by Lewis Brandon himself an important participant in the Sit-ins. To use Sister Alice Walker's definition, they were engaging in "outrageous, audacious, courageous and willful behavior" as womanists do. They were determined to "run on and see what the end would be."

CHAPTER 6

"THE BLANKET OF FEAR WAS LIFTED BY NEGRO YOUTH"[4]

"It was the girls who supplied the fervor and kept the movement going where it had slowed down."
Miles Wolff

It is difficult, perhaps impossible, to know exactly what the numbers of students were and what the exact truth of the events surrounding the Sit-ins is because the participants were not concerned so much about the "facts" and often did not know or care about the identity of those they observed. Being deeply involved in an event like a Sit-in and a march, which can be very intense, takes on its own reality made up of reactions, strong emotions, and perceptions. That said, we can only depend on the statements given to us and the accounts written and try to give a report that is as close to accurate as possible.

As I have stated, the foundation was being prepared for the activism of Bennett Women well before 1960. In 1958, Deloris Tonkins Dozier and a small group of Bennett women began meeting on the campus to plan boycotting the Carolina Theater because of its segregated seating policy. Although the plans did

---

4 Martin Luther King, The Trumpet of Conscience

not get very far at this time, this is nevertheless an indication that the spirit of resistance was finding fertile soil at Bennett College. 5 In October of 1957, Dr. Edward Edmonds, Bennett faculty, had defended the NAACP from a charge of extremism in the *Greensboro Record*, saying that the methods of the organization had always been moderate (see appendix).

Also in 1958, the same year that Martin Luther King came to Bennett, Dr. Warren Ashby spoke at Vespers in the Bennett chapel in May. Invited to do so by Player, he was quietly working on integration with several Greensboro citizens. Dr. Player had expressed the position she took that Bennett should not be in racial seclusion. Many White speakers came to Bennett on a regular basis, local educators, and ministers as well as academic leaders and presidents of colleges from all over the country. Player reported in her interview with Pfaff that White women on the Board of Trustees helped keep Bennett College from being racially isolated, by bringing meetings of people from many different states, "so that it could never be said that the campus was isolated from exposure to other races and groups" (Pfaff, Player interview, 22). Player would continue this practice in 1964 by inviting among others, Dr. Frank Porter Graham, United Nations Moderator, who said that he was "proud that the Sit-down demonstrations against segregated lunch counters had their origins in North Carolina." He called states rights and political monopolies "two great barriers toward complete human equality" (30 May 1960, *Greensboro Daily News*). Player also invited Ralph McGill, a controversial, liberal, White newspaperman at the *Atlanta Constitution*, to speak at the Homemaking Institute with the theme relating to "the current problems in the adjustment to social change" (Player papers, 18 Sept, 1964).

Dr. King's speech at Bennett had been given in February 1958. He undergirds the move to activism in his speech, and

---

5 See the complete story of this effort in the chapter, "Voices of the Belles," Deloris Tonkins Dozier's statement.

challenges the students to be "maladjusted to the injustices of the social order." This was noted by a reporter of the student newspaper, the *Bennett Banner* (Feb. 1958). "You must rise above the narrow confines of individualism to the broader challenge of all humanity," he stated, admonishing the audience that "survival depends upon the spiritual brotherhood of all the world" (*Banner*, Feb 1958, 1). Furthermore King comments on the fact that the ballot is one of the major instruments "the Negro must use to attain his rights."

The same month of Dr. King's visit to Bennett, Dr. Player published an article in *The Methodist Woman*, entitled, "Fellowship without Barriers" calling on Methodism to become racially inclusive. "We [Methodists] must do more to secure broad participation and a sharing of leadership responsibilities without regard to race, color or nationality" (p. 18).

In May of 1958, the editor of the *Bennett Banner*, Carolyn Brown, exhorts her classmates to vote in her article, "A Nation Worries, A Campus Studies":

> "*A few months ago our chief concern and worry was that of Racial (sic) issues developing and arising in Little Rock, Montgomery and Tuskegee....Be prepared to march to the polls. Take advantage of your education, meanwhile the struggle for human dignity moves in the background with cries and muffled voices*" (Banner, May, 1958).

As things continue to heat up in the country and in Greensboro, a Bennett Belle, Roslyn Cheagle, writes an article for the *Banner*, in 1959, entitled "Where Do You Stand?" We know that in 1960, Roslyn was sent to the national NAACP conference in St. Paul Minnesota and that she was later elected a state officer of the Organization of College Chapters (*Banner*, Oct, 1960). We also know that she was a major participant in the Greensboro demonstrations. "Very few persons are successful in trying to play the middle ground when the problem of civil rights is presented," she writes. Roslyn Cheagle's thoughtful and challenging article puts the issues squarely in the lap of her classmates:

> *Do you go downtown and pay for a "crow's nest" seat in the movie? When entering a department store are you guilty of looking for signs which say one race or the other? If we do this we are simply promoting segregation. When you are located near a Negro business do you avoid it and patronize another? Are you guilty of buying food at five and dime stores and standing up and eating it? Why buy food and eat in the middle of the floor? If you can't sit down and eat like other people, let them keep the food. When going home for the holidays will you enter the front door of the station or will you go to the side door and "holler" for a ticket? When boarding the bus will you rush to the back of the bus..? When you and your friends are discussing the possibility of entering an interracial job do you say, "I am not interested"? Are you guilty of Uncle Tomism? by saying "Yes Mam," or "Yes Sir" to someone who does not care two cents for you? Do you stand up to your rights as an American citizen? Are you proud to be called a Negro? When important meetings of the NAACP are being held do you say....I just can't make it tonight? In this progressive age every Bennett girl should answer these questions while traveling home for the Christmas holidays (Bennett Banner, digitalnc.org.)*

At the meeting where Ms. Cheagle and her classmate Joenelle Brown were elected as officers, the College received a plaque in recognition of the voter registration drive, Operation Door Knock conducted in April, 1960. This campaign put nearly 1,000 new voters on the city's books. Bennett students received a citation for outstanding community service from Lane Bryant Annual awards ("Bennett Students Door Knock for Voters Paid Off," Bennett Scrapbook, digital NC). The speaker was Jackie Robinson who commended the student leaders for their Sit-in activities and stated that his lot as the Negro pioneer in major league baseball was "comparatively easy to the lot of the leaders of the Sit-ins." He also stated that the youth displayed amazing strength and maturity in withstanding tradition, social and even parental pressure in some cases" (Banner, Nov, 1960).

In his interview with William Chafe, Hobart Jarrett, activist professor, and advisor to many Bennett women during the movement, describes some of the activities of Bennett College that he had experienced:

> *I remember such things as water fountains....There were Bennett students who refused to drink as I refused to drink out of fountains that said, "For Colored," and eventually those signs came down. One of the remarkable things about the change was the fact that Bennett and nobody else took upon itself the problem of registering Black people.... It was glorious to see... Greensboro Negro people saw something they had never seen in their lives: long lines at the community center...actually waiting in line in a long line in order to get in and be registered. It was as strong a community project as I had I seen. And the city school people and the laboring people everybody fell right into it. We even offered transportation to people to come and get them to go to register (Chafe interview, Civil Rights Greensboro).*

On the November 1960, the *Bennett Banner* published the following statement making its position clear in the matter of the civil rights demonstrations taking place throughout the country:

> *"This letter comes to announce to the general public our views and beliefs concerning the demonstrations taking place throughout the South. We denounce emphatically any barriers that are established to deny full rights to Negroes or other minorities in our society. Therefore we feel that those Sit-ins with specific reference to the Atlanta demonstrations are necessary, even though many persons suffer inconvenience and hardship." Bennett College*

Chapter US National Students Association (Banner, Nov, 1960, 3).

Also in the November 1960 Banner, student Carolyn James comments on the need for action and individual responsibility in her article, "As I See It":

> The structure of society will not change until the Negro exerts all of his powers to finally overcome the indignities he encounters throughout the US each day...The time is now for the Negro to take his own stand on his 'rights' ...practical application in everyday life is one method that the Negro does not utilize...Action rather than words is the only effective way in our modern society. We must all be united in our discontent if progress is to be made. No government is going to grant rights to us. They must be demanded through action rather than words (2).

In President Willa Player's papers we read a letter from Ms. Vivian Mason, public relations consultant from Norfolk, Virginia (see photo in appendix). She makes reference to the Operation Door Knock voter registration drive:

"The voter registration project to be carried out by Bennett is a most exciting movement and you may be starting something that will spread to all our colleges in the South...at least that is my fervent wish." This letter came in the midst of the campaign to integrate Woolworth as it was only a month and a half after the February 1st Sit-ins. Player responds to Ms. Mason on March 15, speaking of "these difficult days"(Player papers).

All of these examples, especially the ones from the College newspaper, indicate a campus that was fully aware and tuned in to what was happening outside the brick walls that surrounded it and also aware of the significance of the winds of change and the importance of developing a mind set that would result in political activism in spite of the attitude on the part of some that Bennett was elitist. There was no ivory tower mentality at Bennett College and no town-gown split with the community. Even more important, the students were examining and struggling with their personal responsibility in the light of these societal changes and during these "difficult days."

With the long reach of time, it is inevitable that our memories confuse and muddy the exact sequence of events. For this reason, it is important to recall the fact that there were two stages to the 60s Civil Rights Movement in Greensboro. The first stage was the lunch counter Sit-ins and the desegregation of Woolworth. The second stage consisted of the mass movement to extend the desegregation to all public accommodations in the city, which focused mainly on restaurants, and movies. This second stage took place mainly in 1962 and 1963. The two stages are related but different. The second stage was directly the result of the inspiration and success of the Sit-in activity. Yet, it was different in that the students were joined in great numbers by the adult community of Greensboro for negotiations, marches, and demonstrations. As time has gone by, popular understanding has often combined the two stages as "the Sit-in movement of Greensboro." It is more accurately referred to as the Civil Rights Movement of Greensboro that lasted for almost four years.

Especially in reviewing the Bennett story and the civil rights struggle in Greensboro, it is important to make the distinction between the two stages of the movement. Once Woolworth was not the focus of the movement, and the student population had changed somewhat due to the graduation of many of the participants, new students came on board, and the momentum of the efforts had to be rekindled. CORE sent representatives to Greensboro and a Core chapter was formed during this period. According to Jibreel Khazan (Pfaff, 164), the CORE group (students and Greensboro adults) was almost entirely different from the group that had been active in the spring of 1960. The initial excitement of the success of the lunch counter efforts gave way to answering the question, How are we going to inspire people to continue this race?

Therefore, we want to understand what Bennett's role was in stage one and in stage two. What follows is a brief summary of events and reflections that give us a view of Bennett's role during both periods. In our last chapter "Voices of the Belles" we will hear directly from the Bennett veterans of the movement.

STAGE I:
THE LUNCH COUNTER SIT-INS

*"Are you guilty of buying food at a five and dime store
and standing up and eating it?"*
                                    Roslyn Cheagle

According to the documentation of Lewis Brandon, ("Sit-in Movement", unpublished MS, 1995), twenty-seven men and four women were present at the counter on February 2, the second day of the Sit-ins. There is no documented record of what school the four women were from. On February 3, students from Bennett College, Greensboro College, and Dudley High School joined. One of the characteristics of the Civil Rights Belles was their dedication to their academic work. Newspaper reporters recorded the fact that Bennett students carried their books in their arms, and read as they sat in. This was because they understood from the administration and their faculty their responsibility to be scholars as well as activists.

A total of 63 students were present by Wednesday, February 3rd. February 4th, and 5th, saw totals of around 300 demonstrators. On February 6th, 400 to 500 students from A&T and Bennett participated in the demonstrations.[6] Let us be clear about the risks these students were taking. Not only were they

---

[6] For a detailed account of the local events surrounding the lunch counter sit-ins, see: William Chafe, *Civilities and Civil Rights* (New York, 1980).

challenging the powerful White establishment and business world, they were often not sure what their parents would say or their teachers. There was much for them to be nervous about.

Miles Wolff *in Lunch at the 5 & 10*, (p. 39), says that large numbers of the student bodies from A&T and Bennett were participating. He does not give a source. He does not say how he knows this. The first time Wolff mentions Bennett women being present at the counters is February 3. These two accounts are contradicted by Gwendolyn Mackel Rice, at that time, a Bennett student, who says she was in the store on the first or second day of the Sit-ins, as the plan had been for Bennett students to be there as observers on the first day, presumably buying items, and serving as potential witnesses. Suffice it to say, Bennett was represented early on.

On April 21, forty-five people refused to leave the counter and were arrested at Woolworth and Kress. Thirteen Bennett students were among them. Khazan gives his opinion of Bennett's participation in his interview with Pfaff: "During that time in 1960 and all through the decade they [Bennett students] were more organized than the students at A&T.... They were involved from the first week of the movement" (Pfaff, 164).

In 1990 Miles Wolff attended the 30th anniversary of the Sit-ins and reported that the A&T Four seemed to realize that they stood on the shoulders of many others. They spoke as "symbols of community, of people working together for change" (Wolff 196-7).

According to Gloria Jean Blair Howard (Bennett class of 1964) Bennett students have not received adequate recognition: "I don't think that the Bennett College students have received recognition that they deserve for participating in the Greensboro movement—Roslyn Cheagle, Jean Franklin and Marilyn Mackel. Bennett had a variety of students from all over the country. There was quite a focus on what we women could do as a group. Bennett College had a lot of women who were going to become doctors and attorneys in a world where women were not supposed to be doctors and attorneys…."(Pfaff, 133).

Bennett's Student Government President Gloria Brown, along with Edward Pitt of A&T, co-chaired the Student Executive Committee for Justice, which served as the planning committee for the demonstrations. Gloria Brown worked closely with Willa Player during the Sit-ins that spring meeting with her at the end of every day's activity. The forward looking and groundbreaking attitude of the College surely had something to do with their willingness to put themselves on the line for social justice. Obviously, what was called a conservative college was only conservative in style not in philosophy.

Jibreel Khazan mentions the summer of 1960 as a time when someone had to maintain the momentum of the movement, and Dudley, Bennett and A&T students who lived or remained in the city were key to keeping efforts going until July of 1960 when the counters were opened (Pfaff, Khazan interview 141).

Joseph McNeil states, "The thing that probably disturbs me the most is the fact that enough people don't get credit for what they did, particularly the females who were the spirit of this movement" (Pfaff, McNeil interview 123).

However Miles Wolff leaves anyone interested in Bennett's role frustrated. One glaring example of his tendency to overlook the College is this statement: *The thirtieth anniversary was much larger than the first two. All the institutions* (italics mine) that were involved in 1960- the city of Greensboro, Woolworth, A&T State University — welcomed the attention and three days of events were held" (Wolff, 910). It is this facile overlooking of the importance of the Bennett contribution that has contributed to the invisibility discussed earlier.

This inaccuracy and other statements like this must contribute to the misconceptions of citizens, but they pale in comparison to Franklin McCain's telling of this story made to a *Greensboro News and Record* reporter for the website interview on www.Sit-ins.com in which he denies the fact that Bennett was involved in the planning of the Sit-ins at the outset and he speculates that Dr. Willa Player would not have allowed her students to participate had she known about the planned Sit-in. Based on his guessing he states: "I doubt that Dr. Player would have permitted that. *Between us guys,* (italics mine) I think she would have talked them out of it or sent them home. The honest truth is the Bennett girls had no idea what we were going to do and neither did Dr. Player. We never once had a conversation with them. The only way Bennett got involved was after the UNCG girls. Bennett girls came after UNCG about say five or six. Bennett girls had no such plans ever" (*News and Record* site: www.Sit-ins.com.audio).

It must be said that these statements directly contradict what Willa Player herself reported to me in 1993 as we talked about the Bennett women and the Sit-ins. At that time she recalled the decision she had made to ask Bennett College students to wait until Christmas break of 1959-60 was over (January 1960) before sitting in so that the break would not stop the momentum of the movement. (Interview for *The Long Walk*. Brown, 1993). Had the Bennett girls not had any such plans, she could not have had this conversation with them or their faculty advisors. With all due respect Mr. McCain's "honest truth" is only the honest truth in his opinion, which was not based on even one conversation with Dr. Willa Player, whose commitment to civil rights activism and role of support for her students has been very well documented

Luckily for us and for history, there is another story told by several people, among them the Rev. John Hatchett who taught and served as Bennett College chaplain from 1958 to 1962 and who advised the College chapter of the NAACP. In an article entitled, "Hidden from History: Bennett College Women and the Sit-ins," published in 2005, Hatchett chronicles his involvement with the Sit-in planning of the Bennett College women. According to Hatchett:

"*This is the untold story, hidden ignored, distorted, falsified and denied by the media....The members of the*

Bennett College NAACP chapter were unequivocally opposed to racial injustice....From September until early November we met constantly and discussed viable strategies to implement our goals....*Just prior to Thanksgiving recess we shared our plans with Willa B. Player* (emphasis mine)....The long Christmas recess was only a little over a month away....With the support and blessing of Dr. Player we decided to include the students from A&T in our discussions....In a series of nightly meetings we met discussed, debated, refined and finalized our strategies....It was agreed that somehow between Christmas recess and the return of the Bennett women to the college the students from A&T would put our idea into execution and we would support them upon our return. Included in the contingent of students from A&T were all four of the young men who were destined to become the Famous Four...What occurred on February 1, 1960 was not the result of a casual dormitory conversation on the campus of A&T College It was the culminating point of an idea rigorously thought through, meticulously debated and refined by a handful of courageous young women on the campus of an all women's college where learning and social activism were inextricably intertwined and endorsed (Hatchett, 2-4).

In an interview with Pfaff in 1989, Rev. Hatchett explained:

The idea that those young men were the sole initiators and the major participants in the Sit-ins is inaccurate but we weren't surprised by the statement that was made. But in order not to create any confusion about what was happening, we agreed we would not say anything about the role we played...in order not to create any conflict between the women at Bennett and the young men at A&T....It was very difficult at that time to get the bulk of the students at A&T to participate. So the young women at Bennett carried almost the full brunt of those day to day *marches in front of the Woolworth store (Pfaff, Hatchett interview74-78).*

The contradictions in these two accounts speak for themselves and teach us much about how history can be so easily misconstrued. The voices of the Belles who witnessed for history between 1960 and 1963 make it clear that they remember well what they did and why they did it.

After the first tumultuous week of the Sit-ins there was a break on February 6 due to a bomb threat. Demonstrations resumed on April 1. During that period, the testimony of a young White woman of Greensboro College, (now Patti Gilbert) who participated on the picket line on one afternoon, gives us an interesting window on the Bennett women she was observing: I have never seen anything like those Bennett Belles," she observed, "they knew who they were. They were upright and the carried themselves with strength. I will never forget them" (Interview with Linda Brown, Dec 11, 2011).

The Bennett women expressed themselves in other ways as well. On February 8, 1960, a junior at Bennett, Karen Myles Leach, had her words published on the opinion page of the *Greensboro Daily News.* She starts out:

I am a Negro and I am proud to be one, because of the contributions that have been made by my race to America. What does the White man fear? Is it that if the Negro is given equal rights which are due him the White man will have too much competition? As a group of human beings of flesh and blood we desire equality. Why is color so important? The heart, mind and soul, aren't these things important? Is there any difference in color here? If so please some one show it to me....I must say that these prejudiced people are non-educated and must realize that what they think is hardly important because....the Negro race is going to take a stand and be recognized for this is the ultimate goal (Greensboro Daily News, 8 Feb., 1960).

On March 31, 1960 1,200 students from Bennett and A&T resolved to put pickets outside variety stores in Greensboro (Chafe, 130). The protests and demonstrations escalated. On April 5 Woolworth and Kress closed. On April 22, the 45 students from both A&T and Bennett were arrested. As a result of sustained efforts of Dudley High School students, under the leadership of William "Bill" Thomas, and with the assistance of Bennett and A&T students who were in town for the summer, efforts of the integration of the lunch counters was accomplished on July 26, 1960.

And so began a lull in the storm, and a kind of transitional period in 1961, with sporadic picketing of Greensboro businesses by committed students. Total desegregation of Greensboro's public accommodations would take two more years of hard work.

Piecing together a completely accurate picture of Bennett and its students' involvement is nearly impossible but when all the fragments are carefully examined, it is very clear that the role of the College was one key to the success of the breakdown of segregation in Greensboro and of the movement that "will justifiably be seen as the catalyst that triggered a decade of revolt— one of the greatest movements in history toward self determination and human dignity" (Chafe, 98).

STAGE II:

THE MASS MOVEMENT

We have tomorrow
Bright before us
Like a flame

Yesterday a night-gone thing
A sun-down name.

And dawn-today
Broad arch above the road we came.
We march!
Langston Hughes

Following the success of the lunch counter Sit-ins, the campaign to desegregate the many public venues in the city took stock of its resources. There were only so many demonstrators available. In the natural evolution of a movement, people get burnt out. Some students graduated and left the city. During the fall of 1961 and up until events began to galvanize the public again, a small but faithful group of people continued to struggle by planning, demonstrating, marching on movies, restaurants and other venues where discrimination was the rule. Of course this included practically all businesses.

Bennett College quietly went about sponsoring activities that would plant seeds of positive relations. For example the campus welcomed White exchange students from Mount Holyoke and Barnard College, as well as many White guest speakers. The

Bennett Banner published an article by Gail Cohen who was an exchange student in 1962. She reported that a Bennett student said to her:

> *'You've probably never seen so many of us at once.' I laughed, but in thinking about it later I realized that it was probably true. I also realized that being in a new situation had changed some of my ideas. Before the exchange program I was very conscious that I was going to a Negro school. I expected the issue of race to be foremost in the philosophy of the school and the thinking of the students. I did not find that to be true. The girls I met were first of all young women in college and the fact that they were Negroes was secondary. When I saw this I think I lost much of race consciousness of my own. I began to feel not so much that it was a Negro school but I was simply at another college (Banner, Feb, 1963, 3).*

We can conclude that the experience of the exchange program had brought her awareness of her own racial attitudes to another level. A Mount Holyoke student wrote about her experience at Bennett:

> *As an outsider at a northern school I have been constantly impressed with the thoroughness that all the students have thought about and understand what must be faced in bringing about integration. Not only do these students discuss the problems privately but they also seem willing to publicly express their opinions and discuss the problem in a well balanced and articulate way (Banner, Feb, 1962, 3).*

Jebreel Khazan in remembering the level and quality of participation of the Bennett Students connects their level of participation to Willa Player:

> *"The reason there were more Bennett students [in the CORE chapter] was because the Bennett girls had as their model Dr. Player. She was a very independent person in her capacity as president. Bennett was a private college*

and there were young women who were leaders in their own right before they ever joined the movement.... They were a small group and they came from various parts of the country, north and south... and they had been told that they were the elite among the Black female students. These young women at Bennett had a banner to carry. If in fact if it had not been for those students at Bennett College we probably would not have had a movement like we did in 1963 because they were steadfast all of the time (Pfaff, Khazan interview 164).

Khazan brings us to the involvement of CORE and Bennett College during the 1962-64 activities. In the spring of 1962 The Freedom Highways project of CORE had pinpointed Howard Johnson's restaurants and Hot Shoppe restaurants along the eastern seaboard.

There was a Hot Shoppe in Greensboro. Khazan reports that the Freedom Highways workshop was held at Bennett because of the leadership of Willa Player. "She was a nationally known educator and she was respected throughout the nation by other educators as well as those in Greensboro, business and political leadership. Her attitude was: as long as you obeyed the administration rules and respected all involved she had nothing against having a CORE meeting there. However it was important that you not do anything to bring a negative image upon Bennett's campus" (Pfaff, Khazan interview 163).

Francis Herbin, in her interview with Pfaff, expresses the opinion that Bennett played a major role in the movement at this time. "I would say that over the next two years [1962-64] much of the support of the movement shifted to Bennett College due to the quiet encouragement of Dr. Willa Player and the student body there although we received support from individuals in the A&T staff" (Pfaff, 168).

The Rev. Tony Stanley, Bennett faculty, and activist describes the Bennett students as "quite militant" in 1962.

"Far more distrusting of the system and the people who claimed they could make it work than in 1960. To them the proof of one's commitment was in what they accomplished. As a result they became totally disillusioned with Ed Zane [businessman and city leader] because he had not done more to further desegregation in 1960....They were supported by more militant Bennett faculty members who were advisors to the chapter [of CORE], Elizabeth Laizner, John Hatchett and the Rev. James Busch" (Pfaff, Stanley interview 162).

Bennett student Lois Lucas was an important member of the CORE chapter. Rev. Hatchett describes her as "very perceptive and aware" (p.153). At this time Lois represents a "bridge leader" as I described them in the chapter "Patterns of Progress." "There was not much activity going on," she says, "until we participated in CORE'S Freedom Highway project. I just did whatever there was to be done. Providing transportation, making placards and picket signs, canvassing neighborhoods to encourage people to register and vote and distributing literature about aiding our boycott of downtown businesses that had begun during the Sit-ins" (Pfaff, p. 155).

Gloria Jean Blair also served as a bridge leader helping to sustain the CORE chapter and the motivation. "In 1962 of my sophomore year at Bennett I attended meetings in the basement of St. Stephens's church. Initially only a small number of students were involved. They were the ones that actually put their bodies there. I picketed the businesses downtown. I also telephoned a lot" (Pfaff, Lucas interview 145). The CORE chapter kept the spirit of activism alive between 1960 and 1962. A&T student Robert "Pat Patterson" served as vice-president of the chapter. He says Bennett women played an important role and names Regina Carpenter and Patricia Murray as members. "Oddly enough the Bennett girls got involved a whole lot earlier and were more actively involved in the Civil Rights Movement in Greensboro than the fellows and the girls at A&T. There were only about 15 or 20 of us [CORE members] at first, basically a few fellows from A&T and a lot of girls from Bennett College and a few people from the community" (Pfaff, Patterson interview 155).

The aim was to open public accommodations to all citizens. The methods used included a boycott against selected downtown merchants as well as marches and requesting service at segregated establishments. The Bennett Banner recorded the "new" aspect of boycotts and marches in December of 1962. By late September, however, hundreds of demonstrators were picketing the S&W and Mayfair cafeterias. On October 13, picket lines gave way to successive Saturdays of mass marches. The *Greensboro Record* reports that virtually all Black ministers in town had gone on record that they were for pushing for integration (Oct. 26, 1962). Fifteen students marched in the first mass march that fall and 2,000 were in the second march. According to Chafe, virtually all Bennett students and as many as half the A&T students took part in the parades. (Chafe, *Civilities*, 112). They demanded a boycott of White merchants who refused to integrate.

Forty-eight members of CORE, led by William Thomas and two Bennett faculty members were arrested for sitting in on Thanksgiving. The *Greensboro News and Record* reports that sixty were arrested at a Carolina Theater and Mayfair Cafeteria demonstration on November 22, 1962. Of those sixty, 38 were from Bennett including 2 faculty members (*Greensboro Record*, 23 Nov. 23, 1962). Lois Lucas, Bennett student, describes one interesting incident during this demonstration:

> It had been two years since the Sit-ins....The only places that had opened up were the Holiday Inn and the Hot Shoppes....There was a Bennett student who spoke fluent French and she put on an African headband. Since she was speaking French the S&W management thought she was an African exchange student and they let her in, but not us. Then she told them who she was and asked if she could

*go in why couldn't the rest of us go in? Once they realized
who she was, she was asked to leave....We really thought
that by being Thanksgiving day and there being so many
of us, that the S&W would be so glad to get the money,
that they would let us eat but it didn't turn out that way
(Pfaff, Lucas interview 194).*

The group was arrested and a number of students went to
the Carolina Theater as well where they were arrested. By three
days after Thanksgiving three or four hundred people were in
jail, some at the armory, due to lack of space.

The 1962 demonstrations can be explained by the lack of
progress in the city since the two years that had passed following
the desegregation of the lunch counters. The students, largely led
by those active in the CORE chapter, felt the frustration of
progress toward equality grinding to a halt. As Chafe put it, "It
was the young people who provided the cutting edge of protest"
(*Civilities*, 110).

Following the mass marches the Executive Committee
waited for the mayor's committee report, which when it came
was disappointing and non-committal. It resulted in no real
progress. Voter registration drives, boycotts, and picketing
continued. In March of 1963, a meeting of CORE was held in
Pfeiffer Hall on Bennett's campus where resentment was
expressed at the lack of movement on the part of City Hall.
Later, in 1964, The *Bennett Banner* would print a summary of the
mood in 1963, by student reporter Frances Campbell:

*January 1963 arrived with a much greater air of intensity.
There was a feeling of apprehension in the air as to what
the New Year would bring. Many Bennett students faced
trials as a result of anti demonstration arrests made before
Christmas. Others greeted the New Year ready to
commence the fight for human rights. The first few months
were relatively tranquil...in the spring the fire exploded
around the world.*

Birmingham was in an uproar... Greensboro also became restless; students met and decided to demon-strate...arrests were made, students were jailed and they experienced the cruel hatred of their fellowmen. Yet they were jailed again and again voluntarily for the cause-never coerced. Our nation as did the world, ended the year [1963] in an air of bewilderment yet not without hope. What was in store for 1964? We can only hope that in such an age of confusion and dissatisfaction Bennett will see its responsibilities and tasks more vividly than before..." (Banner, Jan 1964, 2).

By May 11 of 1963, the CORE chapter decided to picket McDonald's on Summit Avenue. Thirty students picketed McDonald's. There was never any assurance that they would be safe. Some of the students were naïve, but most were aware that they were in harm's way by challenging three centuries of Southern customs and mores. Sarah Jones Outterbridge remembers her participation:

I picketed McDonalds on May 11, 1963...we didn't plan on arrests, but every time we went out into the street we knew that we might get arrested or we might get hurt...we would have the buddy system where you would walk two abreast so that you knew who was with you....we picketed all evening. It was a long, hot evening....It was always frightening because you knew that it was a nonviolent thing. You knew that if someone approached you, you would just stand there; other than try to block a blow, we were instructed not to fight back, so there was always this fear in the back of your mind. I don't remember seeing anyone attacked or hit. They only had a few policemen; police protection was terrible. It was obvious that if something broke out, they might come out or they might

just stand there. We were not sure they would protect us
(Pfaff, Outterbridge interview 204).

This demonstration was the spark that lit the fuse for the largest demonstrations ever conducted in Greensboro. The era of patient waiting was over. For some reason, students, faculty members and adults in the African American community had had enough of the foot-dragging of Greensboro's city fathers and the movement moved into high gear. From May 11 until May 22, 1963, the mass arrests, marches and demonstrations escalated from hundreds to thousands of Greensboro citizens and college students. Large numbers of students were arrested. It is during this period that one could say Bennett truly had its "finest hour."

On May 12, the KKK set up a counter picket line and a can of beer was thrown into the face of a picketer. By May 14, 350 demonstrators had gathered. After Whites threw objects and heckled picketers at the shopping center, the crowd marched downtown to the central business area and held a kneel-in demonstration in front of a local theater (Chafe, *Civilities*, p.121). Instead of allowing themselves to be intimidated, they persisted and raised the ante by praying, but they never knew what the next march would bring.

On May 15, Bennett faculty members James McMillan and Elizabeth Laizner were arrested (*Greensboro Record* "New Moves" 16 May, 1963). They headed up a line of 2,000 students from Bennett and A&T (see appendix) and Greensboro adults who marched to S&W Cafeteria and Mayfair Cafeteria and at the Center and Carolina Theaters (Chafe, *Civilities*, 121). McMillan was threatened by a White bystander with a knife. Holding Dr. Laizner's hand, he whispered to her, "Just keep walking, Dr. Laizner, Just keep walking." (personal interview with author). One night, demonstrators surrounded City Hall and knelt in prayer. On May 16, five White men formed a picket line in front of S&W cafeteria carrying a cardboard sign reading "Niggers go back to Africa" and other derogatory phrases. More than 200

Black students were arrested (*Greensboro Daily News* 16 May, 1963 A1-2).

When we look back we might marvel at their fearlessness. After all, the history of the treatment of Black women and men in Southern jails ranges from verbal abuse to horrific violence, and everything in between. It was no small thing for these students to voluntarily get into a police wagon and be driven off to an unknown fate in a Greensboro jail.

By this time in May it is evident to everyone that the effort in Greensboro to desegregate public accommodations had become a major mass movement. From May until July large numbers of protesters were arrested. The college students were joined by students from Dudley, the Black High School. There were massive arrests on May 17th. It was during this period that over 200 Bennett women were incarcerated.

The May 17 issue of the *Greensboro Daily News* reports that approximately 940 "Negroes" were arrested since anti-segregation demonstrations resumed under CORE on May 11. During one of the marches, Bennett Belle, Sara Jones Outterbridge, was narrowly missed by a knife that someone threw at her (Pfaff, Outterbridge interview 216). On May 18, marchers walked behind a minister and an 18 foot cross. Also on May 18 the Greensboro chamber of Commerce endorsed the "principle of equal treatment of all persons without regard to race color or religion" and urged businesses to begin to serve "all persons of the community" (*Greensboro Record* 18 May, 1963). Still nothing was done.

Hunter Morey of CORE said to a reporter: "It's difficult here. People tend to believe that North Carolina and particularly Greensboro is so advanced that they tend to disbelieve that racial segregation exists here. It's hard to get through to people here. They tend to look the other way" (*Greensboro Record* 20 May, 1963 n.p.). According to the Greensboro Record, Greensboro was the last major city in the state to cling to segregation practices in many areas of business ("Racial Tension Rises," 6 June 1963).

On May 19, the *Greensboro Daily News* reported that 287 people were arrested. They reported that the students used a tactic of circling in front of the cafeteria doors; as they circled they tried to enter the cafeteria (*Greensboro Daily News*, 19 May, 16). The paper described them as "highly disciplined." Arrests had been made on charges of forcible trespass and simple trespass and charges of violating fire laws and blocking building entrances and exits (*Greensboro Daily News*, 18 May 1963). Signs saying, "Go Home Niggers" and "Jungle Bunnies Go Home" printed on them were carried by young Whites. A boy from a car yelled, "Go home niggers you coon."

The students picketed and marched in organized teams. They spelled each other and as one team got arrested, it was replaced by another, and they had their books, always their had their books. At this time the majority of Bennett women were held in the Old Polio Hospital and the armory. Elizabeth Laizner was held with the Bennett students. According to her the officials "stuffed 135 young women from Bennett and A&T and herself into a barracks that was designed for 30 people" Pfaff, 266). Five girls slept sideways on two beds pushed together. The A&T men were in an adjacent barracks. Some of them caught colds from sleeping on concrete floors with no blankets. The girls had no privacy and were forced to undress behind makeshift curtains. Outside the prison some White hoodlums demanded a confrontation with the prisoners. According to the *Greensboro Daily News* about 400 young people were in the Polio hospital at this point.

The students sang freedom songs all night long. The guards threatened to cut off all ventilation if they did not stop singing. "I wish they'd let us run this like a jail," complained one officer. "They've been given entirely too much freedom" (*Greensboro Daily News* 20 May 1963). "The sheriff's guards were a lot nastier than the local police," Lois Lucas remembered, "because most of them were older. Nothing physical just nasty making comments like, 'what do the niggers want now,' and 'Bull Connor really knows how to handle his niggers'" (Lois Lucas, interview, Pfaff, 261). On May 20, the *Greensboro Record* writes that the polio hospital "was pervaded by an air of calmness.... A White CORE worker said, 'there is a large gap between what the sheriff says and what the guards do'" (20 May 1963 B1).

While both colleges pondered what to do, Bennett decided that missed classes would not be considered as cuts. A Bennett College official told the reporter that many of the demonstrators were at the top of their classes and a few missed days would not greatly affect their academic standing. Faculty members had the right to determine the students' grades ("Colleges Ponder Student Problem," *Greensboro Record* 21 May 1963 B1). The students had chosen "jail no bail" as a matter of principal. As long as Black citizens were denied equal access to restaurants, movies and other public venues and as long as the hateful signs "Colored" and "White" remained on restrooms and waiting room doors in Greensboro, they were willing to stay in jail. Roughly one third of the campus was locked up and had a chance to be bailed out but they said "no" we will stay until the walls of segregation come down. As they sang and wrote letters and studied, there was a mass meeting held at Trinity AME Zion church.

What Dr. Hobart Jarrett called "a fighting institution" was revealed clearly during this period by President Dr. Willa B. Player, whose stubborn holding to principle made all the difference for her students. Two hundred of her "girls" were locked up on a matter of justice. She was determined to support them and show solidarity for the cause. Player describes her visit to the jail:

> *I had an anonymous phone call from someone identifying himself as a friend of the College. He said that Bennett students had been placed in the polio hospital without its inspection, which was against the law. I made a personal visit to the library and I read this code. Then I went to visit Captain Jackson and told him about the danger and*

told him...the city could be in trouble. Then I told him unless he agreed to lift the charges against the Bennett girls that they were going to stay out there while I pursued this issue. Then I went out there [to the polio hospital] and told this story to the Bennett girls. I urged them to stay there because Bennett College was not a jail and the administration would not accept them being released into our custody until the chief of police lifted their sentences. They assured me they had no intention of leaving. (Pfaff, Player interview, 262).

Player then sent a telegram to the parents of all the Bennett students who had been locked up reassuring parents that their daughters were safe and being looked after. Lois Lucas remembers this visit:

I can remember Dr. Willa B. Player coming down to make sure her girls were all right. The guards stood up when this regal looking woman came in. If she walked into a prison with some of the worst cutthroats in the world she would command their respect simply by the way that she carried herself. Bennett College's strength was in having been independent with a president and a board of trustees who would stand behind us, having articulate faculty members like Dr. Laizner and Rev. Busch. She came in with words of encouragement. She told us not to worry....Dr. Player made a statement to the press saying our administration was behind us one-hundred percent and she would not knuckle under to any kind of pressure tactics. You can imagine what that did to our spirits (Pfaff, 263).

In the meantime Mayor Schenck threatened to cut off all water supplies from Bennett and A&T if the demonstrations did not cease (Chafe, *Civilities*, 135).

Thomas Farrington, writing for *The A&T Register* remembers one night during the week of incarceration:

All during the night the air was filled with song, mostly led by a group of girls who were next to my so-called cell. These girls had been in this place since the Friday and it was now Monday night. But to listen to these girls you would have never believed this unless you had witnessed this feat for yourself.

While in jail these girls never gave any sign of weariness and they were the ones who really kept the morale high. They actually proved themselves to be stronger then the young men.

The once pleasant night had now grown most unpleasant. Most of the students were adjusting themselves to the situation and were not about to think of giving up (Thomas Farrington, "A Night in the Pen," The A&T Register, 29 May, 1963).

In the meantime the tension continued to build. On Sunday Protestant services were held on the lawn while Sheriff Jones took 70 others to Catholic mass in a bus. Sandra Eccles Sharpe remembers that the officers had the students shackled together and that police dogs came along to the Catholic Church (Brown, personal interview, February, 2012).

Many of those who did not get arrested continued to protest. White and Black girls also picketed at Tate and Walker Streets in front of the Cinema Theater, Apple House, and Town and Campus Restaurants (*Greensboro Daily News*, 19 May).

As mentioned, two of the Bennett faculty members who were very active included Mr. James McMillan, art professor and Dr. Elizabeth Laizner, both of whom worked with the CORE chapter and Bennett students. Dr. Laizner was born in Vienna Austria and had been active with anti-Nazi groups and Catholic students' organizations since she was 16. She had been jailed four times according to the *Bennett Banner*. McMillan would be called upon by Willa Player to get Dr. Laizner out of jail late one night. She had been moved from Greensboro to the High Point jail away from the Bennett students who were incarcerated and as a result of the conditions she contracted a cold.

As the Bennett Belles and A&T and Dudley students sang and studied and wrote letters, a mass meeting was held at Trinity AME church. James Farmer spoke that night to 1,200 people, parents of the students, Greensboro adults, some old enough to be grandparents. He urged the adults to be prepared to go to jail and pick up where the students had left off. The Rev. John Corry, a professor at Bennett, shared his impressions of the situation the students were experiencing at the Polio Hospital. He told the meeting that as many as 75 students had been required to share seven beds in a fifty foot by fifty foot room (Chafe, *Civilities*, p. 130).

The next night, more than 1,000 Black people came together at Trinity AME Zion to support a resolution to boycott White-owned businesses. While the A&T students were released from jail as a result of pressure on Dr. Lewis Dowdy, Bennett women remained in jail for several days due to Dr. Player's stand. On May 22, the largest protest march ever held in Greensboro took place. Over 2,000 people participated in a silent march through downtown Greensboro. On Saturday, May 24, "a temporary truce" was called to make it possible to begin negotiations. Difficult days followed but nothing was resolved. By June 2nd demonstrations started again, culminating in a huge demonstration in what was called Jefferson Square, the heart of the business district. More than 1,000 Black people sat down in the streets on June 6th and filled the jails with their arrests. Finally in the next few days Mayor Schenck drafted a statement that called for an end to segregation of public accommodations. It was a long slow process. "It was only after the 1964 Civil Rights Act that Greensboro reached the same degree of integration that other North Carolina cities had achieved" (Chafe, 149).

It is safe to say that the contribution of Bennett women to this historic struggle was highly significant. With hope, perseverance, and faith, they witnessed for justice, believing that their cause was just and would succeed in the end. Surely they could not know what would meet them in a Southern jail, even Greensboro's Southern jail. Their courage and willingness to endure unknown punishments should stand as an inspiration to all women.

Over 200 Bennett women chose "jail no bail" as an answer to America's version of apartheid. Throughout the struggle they were self-controlled and dignified. They endured racist bullying, spitting, liquids being poured on their heads during some of the marches, and other indignities. Fully focused on their ultimate goal, they did not waver in their commitment to disciplined non-violent behavior. They are magnificent examples of the strength of womanhood at its best and should be remembered and honored as such.

CHAPTER 7

VOICES OF THE BELLES

"You can't unring a "'Belle.'"   *Bennett student, 2011*
"We still hear that drumbeat even now." Esther Terry," '61

In connection with this project, 250 Bennett graduates were asked to answer a questionnaire, give a telephone interview or an interview in person. These are fifty of their responses. They commented on their memories of how they participated in the movement, and how their lives were affected by the experience of having been part of making history in Greensboro between 1958 and 1963. These statements are clear evidence that taking a stand for justice had a powerful impact on their lives and on history. It was a life altering experience for the young women of Bennett College.

Their stories are in turn, moving, poignant, and inspiring, but always revealing of the power and significance of the profound contribution that "ordinary" individuals can make. These were young women who believed in their own power to make a difference for all of America.

Telephone interviews are indicated as well as interviews that took place in person. All other interviews are transcribed from respondents' written answers to the questionnaire. Some editing has been done in the interest of space.

Albea, Hermine Bacote '63

The first Sit-in and the treatment previously given to me and my people as we spent our money downtown motivated me to participate. We were second-class citizens. I participated in the mass movements in Greensboro between 1962 and 1963. At the church service we were told how to act. There were four Bennett women including me that entered the theater at the front door and were about to purchase a ticket, before we were recognized as Black women.

I was able to continue [activism] in my own hometown and become one of the first educators to integrate city schools.

Bartee, Francis Campbell '65

I came to Bennett from Alabama where bus boycotts had taken place just forty miles from where we lived. We had been taught racial consciousness by our parents. In 1963, I joined the fervor of the Sit-in movement. I attended a mass meeting at the church on Market St....Floyd McKissick and James Farmer were our speakers and leaders for the occasion. And the focus that night was on non-violence and passive resistance. We sang songs that caught me up with the fever and made me think that I could take part in something that would change the world for "negroes." I met my husband at that meeting. He was a student at A&T State University....

In November 1963 we [she and her future husband] were among the students who did not leave campus for the Thanksgiving holidays and gladly joined a group who organized to Sit-in at S&W Cafeteria for Thanksgiving dinner. That was my first experience of overt rejection by a group. As we stood in line to obtain a simple meal in a restaurant, I thought about the irony of it all, Thanksgiving, a religious holiday and the treatment that we received. They actually threw their plates down in our direction and walked out. The police were summoned and we stood adamantly where we were as one by one we were escorted out and read our rights as we were arrested and placed in the "paddy" wagon to the downtown jail. We were fingerprinted and placed in holding areas. I became afraid at this point, would we actually be left in jail...This was real. However before the day was over we were bailed by officials of our group.

I didn't know it then but I was lucky, many of my friends in other demonstrations were taken to the county farm and their recounting of their experiences were horrendous. Non-violence was brought home to me when one night as we marched down Market St., a White man emerged from a building right in front of me and elbowed me, leaving me breathless and my future husband who was beside me could only keep walking and fail to protect me.

I remember the songs and the strength that gave us. I often organized groups of my friends in the movement and we sang to keep our sense of direction and purpose. My parents were very supportive of my participation...they had moved to Montgomery and gotten caught up in active demonstrations there. My family marched from Selma to Montgomery with Dr. King and those other icons.

Those days at Bennett influenced the rest of my life and were not the end nor the climax of our experiences...My husband and I returned to Mississippi and he was beaten by a mob who attacked us at a club which we didn't even intentionally integrate. We have used our experiences positively as we have pursued careers and educated our children in a state designated as the "seat of segregation in the South."

Bender, Mary Ellen '60

Attending Bennett including participating in the Sit-ins was a life changing experience for me. I had become aware of discrimination on the campus of Ohio Wesleyan University in the Greek system and the rush there. I was greatly disturbed by witnessing this exclusiveness. This is partly what led me to want to participate in the exchange program with Bennett for the second semester of my junior year. Once at Bennett I enjoyed the smallness of the campus, the sisterhood and my friends there. I asked Dr. Player if I could stay and finish here and was allowed to stay for my senior year and graduate. When the Sit-ins began in February I wanted to go with my Bennett sisters and show my support. Thus began a number of years of working in the Black community including time spent living and working at a settlement house and later time on the campus of Palmer Institute. My experience at Bennett gave me a comfort level in a variety of situations. In all the settings in which I have lived and worked in the last 50 years I have tried to help people of all backgrounds have opportunities and meaningful lives. Friendships formed at Bennett have been important throughout my life.

Blake, Doris Neely '61

I first engaged in social activism in Charlotte where I had joined the NAACP in high school. I was motivated to participate in Greensboro by student friends at A&T who were from Charlotte. I sat in at Woolworth, and the opening of the Woolworth museum was a historic event in my life.

Brown, Linda Beatrice '61

My opportunity to participate in the Greensboro movement came early in the city's civil rights struggle. Before I graduated in '61 I had time to Sit-in at Woolworth and picket downtown merchants in 1960. Of greatest importance to me was that I had taken up the challenge of history and in my own small way said yes to the very serious questions of social activism and racial justice. I was motivated by my upbringing. My father was the Executive Director of the Akron, Ohio Urban League and was on the cutting edge of race relations in Akron. My parents taught us to stand up for what was right at a very early age, and so when I came to Bennett where my mother's sister, Willa Player, was president, I had no hesitation when confronted with a chance to defy segregation.

I had attended my aunt's inauguration as President of Bennett and heard her say: "Ours will be the task of sending out graduates equipped in every respect to help release from bondage a region enslaved with the chains of hate and segregation and to lead forth a people into the full understanding and realization of their rights their privileges and responsibilities as citizens in America's envisioned democracy. At this point there can be no standing still, no compromise, no equivocation." And then during my freshman year she invited Martin Luther King to speak at Bennett. What else was I to do except demonstrate?

I escaped being arrested by a few days, but the experience of sitting at the lunch counter is indelible in my memory. I sat next to my classmate Esther Terry. We were tense, anxious and also excited. Every minute vibrated with the significance of our actions and the risk. I will never forget it. I returned to the downtown on another day to picket and was heckled by White men who drove by in cars calling us names. That was more unnerving than sitting because we were so exposed on the street. I saw some A&T men standing on the far corner for our protection.

These experiences were life changing. They taught me that I had more courage than I realized and that I would never be silent in the face of injustice. They strengthened my ability to cope with and confront the on-going racism and rejection I would experience in my professional life. I went on to become a faculty member at three predominantly White schools, and at UNC-Greensboro I faced and fought a major tenure battle, which was perceived by many as the result of racism. My writing has always reflected my resolve to fight injustice. For 25 years I was an anti-racism trainer and facilitator of workshops, mostly in North Carolina, privately and with the Episcopal Church, hoping to make a difference in people's minds. Yvonne Johnson, a

Bennett graduate, and I gave these workshops together. We founded a non-profit organization devoted to this work. The Sit-in experience at Bennett was my Baptism by fire. I have always been deeply grateful that I was privileged to be a part of that historical event.

Byron-Twyman, Freda Kay Thompson '66

I was born and raised in New York City. I first became involved in social activism in junior high school. I was about twelve years old at the time when I wrote a letter to the mayor of New York City and to the police commissioner. I asked their help in removing the number runners who seemed to congregate on my street just about school dismissal time.....My letter produced results. The meeting place moved around the corner. Action produced results... I attended summer camp in the Shawangunk Mountains of New York....Carlotta Walls and Gloria Ray spent one summer at the camp and shared with all of the campers and staff their experiences as two of the Little Rock Nine. Then being immune to what was happening in the South changed....During my freshman year [1962] some Bennett students and some from neighboring colleges conducted peaceful demonstrations in the downtown area of the city. Movie theaters, restaurants, and stores that didn't admit serve or employ black people were targets for demonstrations. On one occasion while attending a rally outside a local church, a speaker informed the crowd about the arrests of students over the previous few days. He encouraged the group to march peaceably downtown to express its protests against the arrests and the injustices being committed. I listened very intently to all that he said and thought back to a few days before when, or the first time in my life I had been confronted with racial discrimination. After sitting in a restaurants waiting to be served a group of us were told that we would not be served and to please leave. The others in my group complied with the manager's wishes. Although we had been instructed to leave when requested, I could not. I could not understand nor accept what he implied and what I knew to be true. At the insistence of my group leader I left. I was angry, but I left.

It was not anger that prompted me to leave my friends and join the others going into the church. It was a combination of emotions that are very difficult to explain even now. I could say I was feeling hurt frustration, hopeful, but I could never explain the feeling I had. In the church we sang freedom songs and were given instructions should we be arrested. I had not thought about being arrested but apparently others in the group had as some came prepared with small bags just in case.

I was arrested that day after refusing to move from the entrance to a restaurant; I was informed that a law was being violated. And yes, I believed a law was being violated a law which stated that I could, as an American citizen, choose to eat in a place of my choice. I was taken to a makeshift jail (a building which had been condemned by the Health Department) where I was fingerprinted and had mug shots taken. For five days I stayed in a large room with approximately one hundred other females....Our first breath of fresh air did not come until two days after our arrest when we were given fifteen minutes outdoors. Throughout it all our spirits were high....I wrote letters to my friends at school, to friends at home and to members of my family.

When I returned to school I resumed my normal college life, but I was a bit apprehensive knowing that a trial date was to be set and knowing that I might be convicted and that anytime I might be forced to leave school and return to jail. These were realities presented to us from the beginning and I was prepared to deal with them. My trial was never called.

The Civil Rights Movement and the Greensboro movement have greatly influenced my life. I sometimes jokingly remind my husband that he married a jailbird. I regard it as a badge of honor. The demonstrating, marching, singing, the arrest, the booking, the days of confinement make me more appreciative of those on the same journey, those who journeyed before, most of whom I'll never know, and those who still journey today. But the experience, like most experiences in my life, enriched my character and revealed to me who I am.

(The majority of Freda Byron Twyman's statement comes from her dissertation entitled: *Humane Defined: A Definition of Self as Humane Teacher*, published by University Microfilms International, 1979).

Carson, Dianne Mitchell '64

I was returning to campus with a friend. We had been exploring the downtown area which was new to us. We had heard about the demonstration but knew few details when we came upon it at S&W restaurant. While watching we somehow got separated and in the fray I was grabbed and arrested with a group of demonstrators As I looked around the paddy wagon I realized that almost everyone had an overnight bag. We were taken to an abandoned Tuberculosis Hospital [now referred to as the Old Polio Hospital] and booked. We numbered about 250.

The girls were separated from the boys but the rooms were connected by a window...so all of us were kept up with the current happenings. Jesse Jackson was the leader (for the most part) and he kept us informed of what was going on outside.

It was very uncomfortable having the same clothes on for that 4 or 5 days. There was a single commode in the open bathroom. I washed my underwear, but they got lost and I had to endure having none in my VERY short dress. I had to sleep on a table as there were far too few beds. My Bennett friends, back at school finally got a change of clothes to me. We did plenty of singing whenever an official came in –"We Shall Overcome" and others...I later participated in many other demonstrations.

As I look back today I do not regret being arrested that day. It introduced me to the hardship and unfairness many African Americans endured. It was a world I was pretty much sheltered from in DC...those days of discomfort and defiance led me to a new pride in my generation and my race and the realization that because of our actions our children and grandchildren will live in a better world.

Dozier, Deloris Tonkins '58

In the spring of 1957 a small group of Bennett students motivated by the events of the time began meeting on campus with the goal of getting Black people in Greensboro to boycott the then Carolina [Movie] Theater. A film on the bus boycott in Montgomery had been shown on campus and became a stimulus to this group to take action in our segregated community. This was a very short lived affair as our efforts at this time perhaps were too revolutionary for support by A&T College and Bennett administrators. Also, students we approached feared being expelled if they participated in any acts of civil disobedience. Those of us who were involved were afraid of what could happen to us and even were called trouble makers, but we persevered.

We met with Dr. Edward Edmonds a professor at Bennett College who was also president of the local NAACP chapter. He brought to our attention the idea... that Black people should not pay for second-class citizenship. To this end we planned to boycott the Carolina Theater because we were paying to be segregated in the balcony of the theater and we believed it would have economic impact.

During the brief, intense, and fearful period of time the group was active we: held planning meetings in the rooms of Bennett students; placed posters in the student union asking students to meet with us (taken down by the coordinator of student union activities who was aghast at such seemingly out of control behavior); printed flyers inviting others to join our fight against paying for second class citizenship; took flyers to A&T's campus in the hope of getting their students involved...(did not get off the ground); identified some churches to allow us to speak at morning worship and distribute flyers (no takers); and stopped going to the Carolina Theater.

This was an uneasy time. Our efforts did not take hold for several reasons....Greensboro was adjusting to the Brown vs. Board of Education....Whatever the causes, the times were changing, spines were stiffening. Dr. Player was particularly courageous in allowing Dr. King to speak on Bennett's campus in 1958 when other venues refused. Our unheralded effort went no place but I believe it took root and bloomed in season and that it was a precursor to the Greensboro Sit-ins.

Dusenbury, Jacqueline Florance '62

Faculty response at Bennett varied...many warned us about activism. Many of the men at A&T did not want the girls to place themselves in danger. As days progressed, however, participation grew.

Edmonds, Gloria Gilchrist '64

During my freshman year I picketed at various places. I thought it was time for a change. Our leaders told us not to respond towards actions of others. Many of my friends were involved. I feel that the Bennett faculty was indeed in agreement with the movement.. The experience made me less tolerant of those who think they are better than anyone else.

Evans, Joyce Y. '64 (telephone interview, Jan 12, 2011)

Coming to Bennett was my first time in the South. I am from Philadelphia. It was a real culture shock. When I heard about the movement, I got involved. I was excited. Bennett women were the under girding force in the demonstrations at Mayfair and S&W Cafeteria. The men got the credit but the Bennett women were the ones. I enjoyed standing up for something and after the first night I was not afraid. My mother was afraid for me but they were not against it. The experience at Bennett solidified an

attitude in me. I went to the March On Washington, and South
Africa where I visited Robbins Island .

Faison, Charlotte Marie Tenbrook '66

As a freshman I attended anti-discrimination rallies at A&T.
Jesse Jackson was our leader and motivator for change. My
roommate...had been attending the rallies and would come back
to the dorm and talking about how we as students needed to get
involved. She motivated me to attend many civil rights marches
to downtown Greensboro. The Black citizens of Greensboro
showed their support.... I'll never forget when we were
incarcerated in an abandoned hospital. I looked out the window
and saw adults from the community holding hands in a circle
around the building and praying for us. It really uplifted my
feelings. While [we were] incarcerated Dr. Player came to see us.
She said that nothing we would do in life would be as important
as what we were doing now. Then she said that she was proud of
us and not to worry about final exams or class assignments, that
it would be worked out. While incarcerated I called my parents.
They were cautiously supportive. They wanted to know it was
ok. I assured them that I was fine.

When we got to the abandoned hospital the females were on
one side of a long hallway and the males were on the other side.
It was a long dormitory with cots in two long rows. There
weren't enough restrooms for all of us. There was always a line
at the restroom. That first day the left side of my face swelled up
closing my left eye. Several people told those in authority I
needed immediate attention. An officer took me and several of
my friends to the hospital. I remember the White officer saying
he didn't have anything against us and that he was sorry for
what was happening to us. He didn't look much older than we
were. The doctor treated my eye and of course he wanted to
know what was going on at the abandoned hospital. He put this
large white bandage over my eye, which was unnecessary.

Needless to say I got a lot of attention when I returned. People wanted to know, "Who hit you?"

I remember having talent shows in the hallway between females and males. The proceedings were carefully watched by the officers who eventually ended the shows. I guess we were having too much fun.

A Bennett student from Waycoss, Georgia did not participate because she feared that someone from Waycross would see her on television and her parents would lose their jobs. We were told that if we got arrested we would have police records and that we would have a hard time getting a job. I felt I'd cross that bridge when I came to it.

This experience has had a great influence on my life. The idea of standing up for what was right started with my mother long before I entered Bennett College.... My experience at Bennett was an extension of what I saw from my mother. I am proud to have been a part of the Civil Rights Movement. When you are doing something worthwhile there will always be somebody who wants to put up roadblocks to hold you back.

In 1972, I was transferred to a community where few Blacks lived. I was one of two Blacks transferred to integrate the teaching staff. I taught a class of 30 White children. The Civil Rights Movement made me know that I had a right to be at this school and that I was just as smart as any other teacher on the staff....As a retired educator I am still marching for justice. It's in the core of my being....I volunteer in the local schools and participate in outreach programs at church. I'm a better person for the experiences that I've had.

Finger, Dolores '61 (telephone interview, Oct 13, 2011)

Participating in the movement appealed to me because I came from a family that insisted that one take positions. My family was very pleased that I participated. I was arrested in April of 1960. There were 40 of us arrested. They placed us in a holding chamber. I remember I pled "nolo contendra." Dr.

Breathett, Dr. Jarrett, Dr. Garth and Dr. Edmonds were the faculty who influenced me and played a part in my decision to participate. Bennett women were important because we added another dimension to the movement. We approach things differently than men. I had a terrible temper that I had to control while I was demonstrating. One of the A&T men had to quiet me down one day.

Being in the movement influenced the rest of my life. I went to Washington for the 25th anniversary of Brown vs. the Board of Education and took my students. I was a union person. I went on strike with the employees at the Dept. of Social services. I was very much an activist while teaching social work students. I became a member of both SNCC and CORE. Being in the movement in Greensboro has been very important to me.

Grafton, Nannie Hughes '59

I graduated in 1959 and was a dorm director in 1960. I first engaged in social activism when I became the first Black to work in a department store by talking the owner into hiring me. I was shopping downtown when I saw the fellows sitting down. Faculty members did influence me to join the movement. I had some non-violent training.

The bus to South Carolina started in Greensboro. Some Bennett girls and I took the first five seats on the bus and the Whites refused to sit there so we had individual seats most of the way. This activity helped me to clarify and develop values that are still a part of my life.

Garner, Marilyn Frazier '60

I was not a part of the planning but I was motivated by my classmates. Faculty members played a part in my decision to participate. I was advised by faculty members and President Willa Player to participate with pride and dignity. Training took place on campus in the student union. My cousin and his fraternity brothers from A&T participated. This period was very influential in my life. I became more aware of my rights as an American. I am so proud to have seen a portion of the lunch counter at a museum in Washington, D.C.

Harley, Betty J. '61

During my sophomore year at Bennett in 1959 I attended several of the planning meetings. My core principles were aroused urging me to never accept less than equal justice for all. I received training including defensive tactics involving use of hands and arms to shield against spitting and physical attacks. I was part of the first group to protest. Also I worked with the CORE chapter. Bennett women played a pivotal role in the movement as we were among the first to act. I was not arrested. The Bennett faculty, administrators and staff were cautiously encouraging. This period of activism at Bennett shaped my future. I have been a strong civil rights activist throughout my working career and even more during my retirement.

Hawthorne, Willa Pullins '60

I first engaged in social activism in 1960 when I walked in the Sit-in in Greensboro. What motivated me to participate in the Greensboro Sit-in was that the class of 1960 felt it was our personal duty to make changes in the unfair way that Blacks were treated and we were proud of the A&T effort to initiate this change. I received no specific training but we were given direction by Dr. Willa B. Player if we could not do this without violence then do not go....Dr. Player was very supportive and did all she could to be involved with the Bennett women.

I am certainly influenced [by the experience] because I feel that the accomplishment made by myself, my girls and other Afro-Americans made a difference. Without this start we would definitely not have had a Black president.

Jackson, Jean Franklin Michaele '63

I was motivated when I did an internship at Juvenile Services with Claudette Graves Burroughs [7] during the second semester of my senior year, and saw what was going on and the need to get college students involved.

I went with a group to the movie theater and was first to go to the ticket window to purchase a ticket. To my complete surprise I was sold a ticket and went in. "The Wackiest Ship in the Navy" was the movie playing....I'll never forget it. I sat through two shows. Only 2 or three customers came in after me. I understood that a picket line formed soon after I went in and the clerk was quite embarrassed to admit that she sold me a ticket and denied that a "colored person" was in the theater. No one came after me and I finally left after the second showing and joined the outside.

I was arrested and my parents and the faculty were concerned and supportive. We spent two weeks in jail, which was a former TB [and polio] hospital.... On the night we were arrested there were about 400 people processed which included kids under 16, A&T and Bennett students. By morning all the juveniles were removed by Claudette Graves, and after we were finger printed and mug shots were taken they kept all the females in one wing and put all the A&T guys in another wing of the building. After the split there were about 50 females in the space and there was one bathroom and only a few mattresses. Most of us had to sleep on the floor until more people were removed...The governor ordered all students from state schools to be removed...We refused to leave because Dr. Player had sent word that she supported the effort...the guards used scare tactics...when word got out that the guards might try to do some harm to the Bennett ladies A&T men organized themselves and formed a 24 hour human ring around the wing where we were

---

[7] Claudette Graves Burroughs was one of the first five Black students to attend Woman's College, now UNC-G. She sat-in at the lunch counter effort at Woolworth.

located so there would be no harm to us. Finally Dr. Player came to the jail and discussed the options with us and relayed that there had been some compromise made with the leaders of the movement and we decided that it was time to leave. I remember a fleet of cars came to pick us up and it was almost a parade as we traveled down Lee Street and back to school.

Bennett women demonstrated in the evenings after classes. I was arrested while trying to enter the cafeteria downtown. This was a planned demonstration because I was prepared (packed a bag) to be arrested. I called my parents and told them what I was going to do and my roommates were also aware. Because I worked closely with the police department during my internship they all knew me. When the people went to the door of the cafeteria the police took them away and put them in the paddy wagon. When I reached the door one of the policemen said he was not going to arrest me since he knew me so I kept losing my place in line. Finally they insisted that they must arrest me and it did not matter whether they knew me or not. The arresting officer said that if I insisted there was nothing he could do about it since ignoring me did not work so he ended up driving me in the police car seated in the front seat to the jail.

This period influenced my initial jobs because I had a "record". I always had to mention it on the applications. This experience was followed by being a firsthand witness to the police brutality towards people in the streets, and being there during the March on Washington when King did his famous speech; Governor Wallace had banned the showing of the event by TV throughout the state. This certainly influenced me. I became involved as a trainer with a lot of racial sensitivity groups when I moved to Maryland.

Jenkins, Ellarene '66

At Bennett when I heard Dr. Martin Luther King speak I promised myself to go further than just a bachelor's degree. I earned my Masters level credits in 1970. I do remember marching in NC from Bennett's campus to the church not far away to hear Mr. James Farmer speak in my freshman year.... Later I wrote a legal brief that Dr. King was not appreciated. The legal brief to the Supreme Court included a demand to acknowledge him more. In the local parade I saw a banner stating "Jenkins here we come"....I am blessed to be a part of this generation of change in social justice.

Jessup, Gladys '59

I was motivated by Dr. Martin Luther King, Bennett College students, local high school students, churches, family and friends. I graduated in 1959 but I returned to Greensboro each Saturday to participate. I had many friends and family who participated. This period influenced me to be supportive and to participate in any change I believe in.

Johnson, Yvonne Jeffries '64
(Personal Interview, March 15, 2012)

I demonstrated at Woolworth and Mayfair cafeteria. I picketed and marched. We were coming from Woolworth to go to the Carolina Theater and demonstrate. Someone threw a knife that went right past me and landed at my feet. They were calling us "niggers." I heard a loud crack and one of the football players from A&T knocked out one of the hecklers. I looked around and the White guy had landed on the sidewalk. We just kept walking. I was incarcerated for 3 days. We sang all night long. We didn't go to sleep, and the guards could not get any rest. We could have gone out the window but we didn't. The thing that was so reassuring was that we knew that Dr. Player would stand up for us. She had our backs.

My Aunt Lil had taught me that I was not to let anybody take advantage of me. This was crystallized by the experience I had during the 60's. My Aunt and Uncle supported me in the movement. My mother was afraid for me. During the summer I was out of town when I found out that my aunt had sat down in the street during one of the big marches, and that the Black professionals had lost their reservations about demonstrating and joined the fight.

Deciding to demonstrate was not a big decision. I didn't have to think about it. I was sometimes afraid but it didn't deter me. It was like we had been shut up in some chamber and someone opened a door. Since then, I have always been a change agent, working to make things better in the community and standing for what is right. This goes back to Bennett because it is steeped in social justice. Bennett brought great African Americans to the campus to speak. When we were able to chip away at Jim Crow it did have a profound impact on all of us.

Johnson, Jewel Merritt '66

I was one of the girls that was placed in jail or arrested in April of 1963. I was in the group that demonstrated at the movie theater. We were arrested for trespassing because we went downstairs and sat in front to watch a movie. We were taken away in paddy wagons.

We spent four nights and five days in warehouses that they took us to because the downtown jails were already filled with many students from A&T. We were in some very horrid conditions. While we were in jail we sang lots of Negro spirituals. We sang "Hold on", "We Shall Overcome" and many other songs to keep our spirits lifted. It was very emotional.

We were very afraid because we didn't know how Dr. Player was going to react to Bennett girls going to jail for helping to integrate the movie theaters. One day while we were in jail we did get a surprise visit from Dr. Player. She sat with us and told us that we had her full support. We were so relieved because we didn't know what to expect from her. We thought she was coming to tell us we were expelled. She told us not to worry because all of our parents received personal telegrams from her[8] telling them not to worry and that the college would be behind us 100%. During our stay in jail we had visits from James Farmer, Martin Luther King, Jesse Jackson, our leader at the time, and Floyd McKissick Sr. who was our lawyer. Lawyer McKissick and others visited us along with other ministers. We had to be fingerprinted the night of the arrest. When we did go to court he [McKissick] was able to get us all acquitted after we went through a trial in Greensboro.

The day we were released from jail after not being able to wash thoroughly for 4 days was a relief. We were served brains and eggs, which no one could eat. We were starving. They had us packed in cells. Men and women were in the same room at first. A request was made to let the girls be placed together and the boys placed in another room. These were fellows from A&T who had also been jailed.

The day that we were released all of our parents had been notified and they were there to greet us with hugs, kisses, food, clean clothes and many friends. The community was there to cheer us on....These were very trying times for us and being a freshman at the time, I was scared but determined to help with the movement. Jesse Jackson had mentioned that he needed the help of the Bennett women and he hoped that we would participate. We did. We were called the Bennett 100 because it was estimated that about 100 girls went to jail. [According to Dr. Willa Player and other sources, the total number of Bennett women arrested and jailed was at least 200]. They were shocked that Bennett girls went to jail. Some teased us and called us the Bennett jailbirds as a slang. The college and community were very proud of us, also our parents. When exam time came we hadn't had time to study so the instructors and the president gave us the option to keep our grade point average.

---

[8] See the appendix for a copy of the telegram sent by Willa Player to the parents.

This period influenced my life immensely. I was always a strong advocate for civil rights and social justice. I attended lots of marches: the 1963 March on Washington; the Poor People's March after Dr. King's death; we marched to make his birthday a holiday; the Million Man March; the NAACP March for jobs, justice and peace. I was the first in my school in Washington DC to teach African American Studies in the 60's. I taught it in every school where I taught school. I was usually the first to teach African studies in each school. I have a strong feeling for civil rights at all times on any level and subject. I love to read novels about African American history. I do not like to see Black people mistreated under any circumstances.

I went on an education study tour of West Africa to study African culture...this was a wonderful experience in our African ancestry and culture. I am a life-time member of the NAACP and the National Council of Negro Women.

The movement has a great influence on my life forever. I love the courage that I developed from this movement and the spiritual caring and healing that this movement gave me, and others. That was one of the best educational experiences that we brought with us into our life's growing period. It was a great feeling to have and a great accomplishment.

Mackel, Marilyn Hortense '65

My first social activism was at Bennett picketing the S&W cafeteria and movies. To me it was the natural thing to do. I did not give it a second thought. I was president of Bennett's chapter of the NAACP. I was active with CORE, and worked with Bill Thomas and his sister Anthonette who was my classmate at Bennett. My teachers at Bennett taught in an activist style. Rev. Hatchett, and the dance teacher who was fired because of her husband's connection with communists was exposed in the press. [9] Dr. Grandison had us doing voter registration and some

---

[9] Accusations of communist connections were considered a major threat.

other surveys so the seeds were constantly planted....Training involved how to respond at each action.

I remember more than a few discussions about getting the men from A&T involved particularly when we expanded picketing to Burger King. Its location raised the bar for danger-there were really few male students involved on a daily basis. I remember specific discussions about getting the football team to protect us — Jesse Jackson its captain. Well it did not happen. Indeed it was after we left for the summer that Jesse and Rev. Stanley led protests that hit the news — as I recall some violence erupted. That was I believe when Jesse finally got involved in the movement— not when we were daily marching, picketing, etc for years! I was arrested and ended up in the polio hospital for a week. Parents and Bennett were totally supportive. Dr. Player was WONDERFULLY supportive and strong. Looking back I am amazed at her fortitude.!

I think Bennett set me on a path of speaking up at all costs. I have just retired and found myself speaking at the judges retirement dinner about not sending judges who don't want to work with juveniles to the juvenile courts...and recommended that every judge read Michelle Alexander's book, The New Jim Crow.

Matthew, Claraleata Cutler '65

I participated in the mass movement in 1963. My sister was at Bennett and she told me about the Sit-ins in 1960. I was arrested in 1963 along with a lot of my friends, and my parents were appalled.

I'll always remember the humility of feeling like I was worthless. We couldn't try on clothes before buying them. We had to use the fire escape stairs to go to the movies. The Whites threw things at us. I attended school in Camden with Blacks Jews and Polish people and we all got along fine so the racism in NC was a real shock!

McCain, Bettye Davis '63   (Interviewed by Dr. Audrey Ward)

During the 1960's I served as a secretary of the College's Civil Rights Executive Board. Girls at Bennett College were marching and I was among them. One night we were locked up. Dr. Player came the next day and she supported us. We were there for three days....We were committed to the cause. I was vice-president of my senior class.

McKie, Carolyn Maddox '66

Almost my entire dormitory was marching. It taught me to be bold and to stand up for my rights. I hoped my marching would make a small impact on history. I grew up in a period of segregation but this move strengthened me. For example my first job was in a newly desegregated school in Burlington, N.C. where I boldly entered the teaching staff as the ONLY BLACK FEMALE. I lived in Burlington in a newly built all white apartment complex. The realtors would not show my husband and me any houses in nice sections of town. I currently live in a predominantly White neighborhood in Chesapeake, VA. When Black friends ask me why we live out here where the Klan used to meet I reply, "because I can." I can truly thank Bennett College for helping me to develop into a strong black woman.

Mims, Judith Jones '66

I participated in at S&W Cafeteria and the movies. Jesse Jackson motivated me. CORE gave us a short session on how to behave. I was arrested and I know I never want to experience that again. Bennett women provided a lot of support for A&T students. This period opened up my eyes to segregation.

Morton, Iris Jeffries '61

"Being at Bennett during the Sit-ins and having an opportunity to participate was one of the highlights of my college education. The intensity with which we gathered behind the Administration Building to be picked up and driven downtown to Sit-in was astounding. We were not jubilant or sad but had a mission. This single mission of challenging social Injustice was a hallmark for many of us in defining ourselves at that period of our lives. What a wholesome impact it made on our characters and principals and what wonderful leadership we had in our president, Dr. Willa B. Player. While sitting at the lunch counter one day, after a grueling chemistry class and prior to eating, a young child asked her mother, "Mama why aren't the niggers eating? The stoic mother replied, "The niggers ain't hungry."

As we were picked up to go back to campus one day and another group of students were being dropped off, a policeman appeared from nowhere and gave the driver a ticket for being illegally parked. As the driver took the ticket, a White middle aged female was passing by and immediately stopped and gave the driver a check. She said, "I hope this will help. I really support what you all are doing."

It was the curiosity and honesty of the children and youth, the compassion and support of the middle aged and elderly that had given many of us hope and had propelled the national cause for desegregation and equality. I am convinced that the legacy that was started during slavery and ignited again in the sixties will always serve as a reminder to the young African Americans of the strength and determination of our ancestors.

Neff, Jean Herbert (attended Bennett as an exchange student her sophomore year- 1959-1960).   Phone interview (Aug 2011; and written response)

I was motivated to participate in the Sit-ins based primarily by the way I was raised. I grew up in a home and faith community (Church of the Brethren). We were pacifists so non-violence was very much a part of my moral upbringing. I was always aware of and deeply troubled by segregation and racial injustice in our country. I identified with the plight of African

Americans and outraged at the shame and horror of Jim Crow laws. Meeting it in Greensboro was shocking and unbelievable. I was also aware of racial prejudice in the north.

So I readily participated in the Sit-ins because it was simply a complete expression of myself, where I was able to give voice (with many others) to a cause that so mirrored my own deeply held views. It was a chance to change the social contract— society itself. It was a high point in my life and a privilege to participate in the Sit-ins....I remember joining other Bennett students very early in February, 1960....there was an explicit supportive atmosphere on campus. The faculty provided a real way of conveying not just that they were behind us, but they were one in this with us. I understood that this was not new to campus life- it was who Bennett was all along. I later learned how early Bennett students were involved in social activism (the 1930's). Dr. Player, Dr. Jarrett, and John Hatchett and others were a powerful noble and eminent presence in my life....

I attended the conference at Shaw University in Raleigh April, 15-17, 1960. More specific directions were given then regarding how to handle oneself in picketing and sitting-in. One-hundred and twenty-six student delegates participated from fifty-eight Sit-in centers. I was not a delegate from Bennett, it must have been that the Church of the Brethren made it possible for me to attend. It was an extraordinary experience to be in a room where Dr. King was speaking. There was such a feeling of being in the presence of great moral leadership and high purpose. I also attended the National Institute on Race Relations at Fisk University in the summer of 1960. It is difficult to express the full meaning these experiences had on my life. I was so wedded to the goals of the Civil Rights Movement.

I was arrested o April 21, 1960 along with the other Bennett and A&T students. We were bailed out on the same day via NAACP Legal Defense Fund money. There was a sense of calm, composure and resolve while we sat in prison. We were in this together and bound to one another.

My father and mother were divorced. My father was very angry about my participation in the Sit-ins and probably more specifically about my arrest. I had not let him know of any of this. He called Dr. Player directly to complain. My mother was concerned for my well-being but was quite supportive. She was in Africa at the time.

I loved being at Bennett. I was friends with a number of students, some of who participated in the Sit-ins some who did not.....It was so important to our nation that we could redefine ourselves to become a more inclusive, fair and just society— North and South. It was a great privilege to be at Bennett and to be able to participate in the Sit-ins. It was an uplifting and prophetic time. It has and will stay with me all my days.

I participated in the March on Washington and in a march protesting the war in Iraq in 2003. It is a lasting gift to me, and all of us that were part of that story.

Powell, Susie Ruth '64

The first night after I was arrested I slept on a wood floor. I was jailed at the Old Polio hospital. I promised my father on his death bed that I would not participate. I waited three years before going to jail. My mother was scared. When a dance teacher at Bennett was fired because she was accused of being communist I was motivated to participate.

Revell, Yvonne '60 Interview from the John Novak Digital Collection, Marygrove College May 28, 2004 tape# o5.28.04-yr)

I did not have a seat at the lunch counter but was standing behind the bar stools. I was frightened because of the White men behind me. They had crew cut hairstyles and they had chains in their hands and were screaming racial slurs. One heckler burned a hole in my coat with a cigarette. Chains were moving behind me. I was there on the last day. Hundreds of students marched down Elm St. There were shouts of joy and relief. "It's all over," they shouted, we can eat, It's all over." I spent time as a youth sewing and would have to buy supplies at Woolworth and would have to wait in line after everyone was finished to pay. I would pass stores that I could not eat in and wondered where I would use the skills I learned at Bennett. My parents were against my demonstrating.

Rice, Gwendolyn Mackel '61
(Interviewed by Carmen Smith, Feb. 9, 2010)

When I came to Bennett I was already interested in civil rights because of my parents. My family was forced to leave Mississippi under cover of darkness because of my father's civil rights activities.

I was active in the NAACP and my senior year at Bennett I served as president of the campus chapter. Several of my professors who were civil rights activists helped to shape our viewpoints and exposed us to social issues. One of those professors was a holocaust survivor who taught economics....

I was among the group of students involved in planning and strategizing the Sit-in movement. I vividly recall meeting with the A&T students to determine the strategy for the first day. The A&T students would sit at the lunch counter and we would be in the store shopping to prove that we were customers and indeed worthy to sit at the lunch counters.

Additionally I was one of the leaders in the effort to integrate the Carolina Theater. Although we were admitted (there were about 5 of us), when other students went down they were barred and integration did not happen rapidly. However the newspapers reported that we were allowed in because we were Eskimos. I guess that's because one or two of our group wore parkas and I wore a camel hair wool coat with a raccoon collar.

(Interview Transcript, Gwendolyn Mackel Rice interview,
Novak digital Interview Collection; Civil Rights Series
June 10, 2011)

We were constantly rotating and going down there, and
then one day they finally arrested us...we were advised by an
attorney...we were booked but we were not kept in jail...But I
remember Dr. Player...she knew we had gone and she called us
into her office, into her home really. And she said 'Young ladies
you get some of those men to go down there with you [to the
theater]. Don't go down there by yourself anymore' So we made
a promise that we would.... {my parents] weren't worried
because they knew Bennett. They were comfortable with us at
Bennett.

**(Carmen Smith interview, Gwendolyn Mackel Rice,
2010, continued)**

I feel that the world has been cheated of knowing the whole
story. As time goes on memory becomes more selective and
unless someone like you and your sister classmates write this
down we will be forgotten. My participation in the movement
made me feel that I was making a contribution to the world, that
indeed I was a young adult and had already taken steps to insure
a better world for future generations. I continue to work for
equity and justice in the work I do now... to insure that people
are treated with dignity and justice. Currently a major effort that
I am engaged in is to [secure?] transportation equity in the city of
Chicago, particularly for residents on the south side.

Riggs, Elizabeth A. '63

My inability to try on hats in department stores, or eat at
lunch counters, and a separate movie entrance motivated me to
participate. Dr. George Breathett and Dr. Dorothy Bardoph,
Bennett faculty, played a part in my decision to participate. They
gave me advice. I received non-violent training at a Methodist
church. I learned how to stand by mute and not react physically

or verbally. This period <u>absolutely</u> influenced the rest of my life. It was very important to my relationship to the world and national politics. I've remained a political activist. It changed Bennett for the good.

I worked in Greensboro for a year. I was Director of Headstart, the Neighborhood Youth Core, Upward bound and OEO. I remained politically active in my hometown Camden. NJ. It propelled my admission to law school...and subsequently appointment [as judge] from Superior Court State of California. I owe my career in law to my parents who though poor <u>made me</u> go to Bennett. I learned how to become a leader at this all women's institution. I believed this occurred because I didn't have to compete with males who had the benefit of their girl friends' support in positions of leadership. It gave me and other women a voice not encumbered, or compromised by male, female relationships.

Roberts, Doris Alston '64

I marched a lot during the mass movement in Greensboro I was spit on and water was thrown on me during the marches. I didn't have a fear of death I was motivated to go through. It was just something about it. I was with friends from Bennett and friends from the church. Dr. Player told us "You have my permission to continue no matter what happens at A&T." My parents marched too....we were just motivated. Bennett women kept it going because Dr. Player gave us permission. She supported us. We [Bennett students] don't get the credit but we kept it going....the marching made me aware we weren't treated right. I saw where it was really bad for our children.

Ryder, Jane A. '65   (Phone interview, April 2012; also written Questionnaire)

By the time I got to Bennett social activism was a way of life. I attended The Rev. Martin Luther King's church and met him before the Bus Boycott. I was about 10 or 11. One summer in Montgomery we walked down the street in the direction of King's house and my sister and I bowed in the direction of his house. We had family discussions about the NAACP and Dr. King. I was still in high school when the lunch counter action took place. As students we boycotted school one day because our school was built behind a prison and stores in downtown New Bern. I participated in every march that was organized while I was in college. I was never arrested.

One thing Dr. Player requested of us was that we attend all classes then get in line to march. The spring of 1962 I had a class that met the last hour of the class day and though I was ever last in line I was close to the end....I had packed some articles of clothing in a large purse just in case I was jailed. But the last student who was taken to jail was standing just in front of me as the jails were declared full when I stepped up the theater window to purchase a ticket.

By their willingness to participate, Bennett women showed their understanding and belief in the US Constitution and their dissatisfaction at how the Constitution was being interpreted and applied to their lives; they showed their acceptance of ...non violent protest and communicated faith and trust in our black leadership. They placed their lives in jeopardy for their beliefs and perspectives on the meaning of equal rights...giving added credence to Dr. King's words: "I submit to you if a man hasn't discovered something he is willing to die for he isn't fit to live." Bennett women were able to see into the future a healthier nation for all people and capture it through present actions. The role of the Bennett Woman has always been that of exemplifying the Phenomenal Woman without being able to consciously predict the profound impact of our actions.

The faculty was very supportive and I witnessed faculty marching everyday that we marched. President Player was very, very supportive. She drove the length of the line with her window rolled down and smiling at us each day that we marched and visited students who were in jail. She sent night letters to parents of students who were in jail letting the parents know what was happening. She met with faculty and staff to explore ways to support students once they returned to campus, and with students who were not jailed to explore ways to support students once they returned to campus. She received an anonymous phone call from what sounded like a White male telling her that it was illegal to house the students in the abandoned hospital and she...confirmed it and was able to negotiate an early release of the students.

After graduation in Houston I taught at a large middle school with many low-income students. I had raised the African American math score about 80%. The administration actively resisted my efforts to do this. The Sit-ins strengthened my resolve. I was straightforward with racist school officials who were very difficult. I risked my job. This and the Sit-ins prepared me for the rest of what I had to fight at Prairie View. Along with other grad students, I lobbied Texas Legislature for state money that Prairie view A&M University had never received. The Texas A&M University system was ordered to pay Prairie View A&M University $6,000,000 a year for ten years.

Satterfield, Shirley Ann '63

I attended high school in Princeton, NJ....I first engaged in activism when I joined the Sit-in at Woolworth in Greensboro. I marched with the Bennett students....through the streets of Greensboro to Woolworth. I remember as we marched there were White people along the side of the road throwing things, calling us name and agitating....I was motivated to be in the Sit-ins because when I was a freshman at Bennett I wore my hat and gloves and had my pocketbook and went to the movie with my junior sister. When we reached the theater I went to pay and she informed me that we had to go to the side entrance where there was a green sign that read 'colored entrance"- we had to sit in the balcony....I do not remember receiving any non-violent training but I remember that when we marched and sat in at the counter we were not supposed to react to hecklers.

I was the secretary of the campus NAACP. I chose not to be arrested because I was worried about a paper I had to turn in for a class; however my roommate went to jail and sent me a letter from jail. Many of my Bennett friends participated.

This period had a memorable influence on me. I grew up in a segregated town- Princeton NJ. I went to a segregated school- Witherspoon School for colored children- until the schools were integrated. When I was in the second grade the "Princeton Plan" was instituted that integrated the two elementary schools in Princeton Borough. In the third grade I attended the elementary school that was all White and noticed the difference in the way the colored children were treated. The town was so segregated that our community had stores, beauty salons and all establishments, because we were not allowed to shop on the main street in Princeton....I knew before I attended Bennett how degrading it was for me and all African Americans to be segregated against. As a student at Bennett again I was faced with segregation. It was expected in the South, but many do not know how prevalent it was in some places in the North, especially in Princeton.

As a teacher, high school guidance counselor and historian of the African American community in Princeton, I often tell the story of my experience with the marches and Sit-ins in Greensboro. After graduation at Bennett I moved to Las Vegas NV to teach in a segregated community and school, traveled from Las Vegas to Princeton in 1964 with two Bennett sisters only to encounter segregated situations going through the southern states....When I visited the wax museum in Baltimore with my church group [where there is a display of the Woolworth counter and pictures] I told them about the Sit-ins and that I was a part of it....There was another school group next to us who was listening and the teacher told the children that they were seeing and hearing from a "legend"!

Sharp, Sandra Echols (Interview in the "Greensboro Gazette,"
Oct 1997

What happened on Wed, May 15, 1963 we can never forget. The big day arrived for the Bennett College demonstration. ...Bennett was the dominant group at the S&W Cafeteria. We used a number of tactics that were taught to us by the leaders of CORE. We walked in a circle in front of the revolving doors. I went inside thinking that the other girls were right behind me, but found myself standing alone face to face with an assistant manager. He said in an angry voice, "You are trespassing on my property!" He signaled two policemen who came into the restaurant. They escorted me outside where a police car was waiting. Soon the Bennett and A&T students were arrested and we were shoved into police cars.

When we entered the compound [at the Old Polio Hospital] incarceration began. The conditions were poor. There was no regular supply of food. We ate at no consistent time. We ate when different churches and friends of Bennett sent us food. The care packages were much appreciated because the quality of food varied. Two Bennett College students and I organized the distribution of food since this was another serious problem....

Bathroom facilities were sorely lacking. The approximately 140 Bennett students used one toilet. There were no showers or baths and one cold water sink provided us with a cold water wash up...We used one phone located near the Sheriff's office. Neither television radios nor tape recorders were allowed...We also lacked sleeping accommodations 29 beds were provided for over 132 Bennett students. Many of us slept on cold damp concrete floors.

We lacked medical attention. Students became ill....My mother [a Bennett graduate, class of '42] disguised herself as a nurse. She wore a White uniform in order to gain entrance to the compound. She sat with us and held us and took some of the sick students to the hospital. After bringing us some things she called Attorney General Robert Kennedy and told him about our condition. We were released under bond and sent back to the campus to await trial. Practically all our cases were thrown out. They could not identify 132 students.

Later I went to South Carolina to work with SNCC and the American Friends Service Committee. My activity in Greensboro prepared me for how difficult it was in South Carolina. I also joined the Peace Corps and spent over two years in Africa.

Bennett College students played an important role in the desegregation of the cafeteria.

Sizemore, Dorinda Smith '66 (telephone interview, 2011)

I was an on-going participant in 1962-64. I was with the group at the movie. We were watching the movie in the front of the theater and the state troopers came in with the dogs. I remember the "padded" wagons. I was arrested, and our parents got a telegram from Dr. Player. A trustee prison guard came in to feed us. Dr. Player sent a telegram to all families whose daughters were participating. My parents were really proud. Martin Luther King came once. State troopers came on a Sunday to take us to church. We were chained and they brought the dogs to church. It affected me because when I returned home I was kind of hostile. My mother's employer told her she was wasting money on my education. When I came back home I was cautious, In the school system I became an administrator. I got the kids involved by telling them about my experience.

Smith, Hazel Elizabeth Abron '63

When not in class I would go to Sit-in. I only carried a sign when someone needed a break. I walked until I needed to return to campus. I was not really an activist or very brave. What I did seemed relatively safe and the least I could do. Raised in the segregated south always rankled, especially the segregated US. I knew that we needed to help especially at Bennett College because we were a private institution. I knew the concept of non-

violence...that we were not to react....I remember being very
upset when I heard that the Bennett dance teacher had been fired
for being a suspected communist. I was always amazed and
proud that I was present as a freshman student in Greensboro
when this very historical moment began.

Smith, Roslyn '61 (Scher, Dena, Novak Interview Digital Collection: Interviewee Roslyn Smith May 12, 2010 Interview # 05.12,10-RS (Audio Digital File).

One of the things we as Bennett students have been trying to
convey over the years is that we were in on the planning at the
beginning....Because in recent years the participation of Bennett
students has been reduced and almost pushed aside....We also
say that history has to be corrected   because it seems that
somehow we are being written out....We were initially going to
picket and at some point we were going to go a step further by
going inside and asking for service at the lunch counter....we
had a date that first week in February; the strategy was that A&T
guys would be our backs so if there was trouble you know they
would be there, but the four of them go down and we didn't
know until that evening. No, I didn't go down the next day
because my picketing had to be arranged around my work
schedule and my study schedule...I think I probably went down
the third day.

Dr. Player felt that if we were going to have a Sit-in
movement downtown that we needed the protection of males.

Smith, Roslyn '61, continued
(Brown, personal interview Oct. 31, 2011)

Dr. Edmonds [Bennett faculty] was the essence of all my
maturing into becoming knowledgeable about our people. He
was the president of the NAACP and advisor to the Bennett
chapter. A cross was burned on his lawn the spring of our
freshman year. Dr. Breathett and Dr. Jarrett were also influences.
I was sociology major. I was Dr. Jarrett's secretary and Black

community leaders were in an out of his office that year. The Homemaking Institutes that were held, especially Operation Door Knock increased our awakening.

During 58/59 school year, we had meetings in the upstairs level of the student union. Officers of the student senate, Gloria Brown, Margaret Bailey, Von Moore, Roslyn Cheagle , Gwen Mackel, Dee Finger- we all met with Rev. Hatchett. We decided we needed to be involved in the movement. It was like, it's your time and you're going to have to seize the time. These were the meetings referred to by Rev. Hatchett in his article. We met every week. At some point the guys from A&T were brought into the discussion. It was before Christmas when Gloria Brown had a meeting with Dr. Player and she had indicated that we should wait until the first of the year to start demonstrating. Gloria came back and reported this to us. That was why we didn't start until after Feb 1.

As a child in Princeton, West Virginia I was aware of how things were. Once a little boy called me a nigger and he ran into the house. I charged up his steps and said, "Who are you calling a nigger?" His mother said she would call the police but nothing happened.

I went downtown the first and second week. I knew what I was getting into. We were trained in how to behave and made picket signs at Bennett. I knew I could not tell my mother, and I didn't tell until that summer when school was out. Dr. Player made a great impression on us. She accomplished so much and made an indelible impression on us. She said we had to know how to conduct ourselves. We had to have a plan. We were not going to cut classes and we were to dress appropriately and not strike back or retaliate.

The Greensboro demonstrations were the starting point for my life changing. I had learned how things were run. After graduation I worked for the department of welfare and social services. I was involved in the NAACP and a political club I went to union meetings and worked in community organizing.

I would like for this book to tell the truth and record the facts about the participation of Bennett women. Our generation needs to do that for this generation. We took a stand and we followed through on it. I would like to say to young people, "We stood up. Are you going to do anything?"

Soublet, Beatrice Perry '65

I attended high school in New Orleans and my first social activism was registering people to vote there in New Orleans. I was motivated to participate in the Sit-ins because I desired social change. I was trained by CORE in non-violent demonstration. I first went downtown to demonstrate on Nov 17, 1962. I was arrested twice but not put in jail. My parents were concerned. I remember that faculty members and Dr. Player were very supportive and positive.

These are pages from my diary:

November 17, 1962: Dear Diary, I sat in today. We went to Mayfair restaurant and were arrested. I rode in the paddy wagon. Package from home. Hat and jewelry.

November 22, 1962; Dear Diary, Sat in at S&W. We got out on $50.00 bond. Tony and I came home to go the movie. I'm tired. White Breakfast. [10]

May 16, 1963 Dear Diary: Picketing and marching in town. Some of the kids may go to jail tomorrow.

May 19, 1963: Dear Diary, Went to High Point to help with CORE material. Went to see the fellows at High Point jail and Polio hospital.

---

[10] At this time the 'White Breakfast' was a Thanksgiving tradition at Bennett. The entire student body dressed in white and celebrated Thanksgiving morning.

May 20, 1963: Dear Diary, Demonstrations, no class. Many kids went to jail. Tony took me to see our house.

May 21, 1963: Dear Diary, Tried to get to jail where many kids are released, Tony, Margie D., Bill T. and I went to Dr. Player's at 3:30 in the morning.

I am still a social activist. I was arrested in front of the South African Embassy in D.C. I demonstrated against the war three Friday's a month. Participating at Bennett did not effect my education. I didn't want to miss my finals my sophomore year because I had been selected to go to Willamette University my junior year.

Stokes, Alma '64 (Interviewed by Audrey Ward)

Some people went to jail. However being a student with a family I did not want to do anything that would jeopardize my family or my education. [She was a wife and mother, ten years older than her classmates at Bennett]....I took my first teaching job in a predominantly White school. I was academically prepared and I knew how to control my temper, which incidentally was put to the test....My kids and I joined the churches and community in the downtown marches, but we were thoughtful and calm.

Taylor, Phillis Strong '64

Born in the early 40's into a family of activists I was given a strong and influential involvement in the struggle for human rights. My maternal grandmother was a member of Marcus Garvey's United Negro Improvement Association. During the late 1930's and early 40's my parents were members of the National Negro Council which opposed all forms of racial discrimination and fought to free, among others the Scottsboro

Boys....In keeping with my activist heritage, I joined the fight for equality and in addition being a participant in the Sit-ins and demonstrations in 1963. During my years as a student at Bennett College these efforts were both accepted and supported by my family......Floyd McKissick was our lawyer handling hundreds of cases daily. John Lewis came to speak with and encourage us as a representative of SNCC. Jesse Jackson was the designated leader for our protests. While we endured the often reported violence denial of rights and were once jailed and were herded into less than adequate cells without the necessary human niceties, the pride, determination and sense of purpose which permeated those dark times were overshadowed by the unity the prayers and more than anything the songs of freedom....

As a professional educator...I involved myself in the extended struggle for community control of the neighborhood schools in Ocean-Hill Brownsville. I fought for better community schools and inclusion of African American teachers in the New York City educational system. I have been a member of several civil rights organizations and have organized voter registration campaigns.

(The following are excerpts from Phillis Strong Taylor's letters to her mother during her participation in the demonstrations in Greensboro in 1963):

Wednesday, May 15, 1963
Dear Mother,
You probably know that something is up because I am writing so soon....Tonight we went downtown to picket. There were about 200 persons arrested out of 1,500-2000 marchers. We picketed two restaurants and two movie houses. The city had no more room in the courthouse and jail for us, so they refused to arrest any more students. I was with the group that went to S&W restaurant. They

had arrested two groups ahead of us, and when it came our turn to be arrested the police did not have enough vehicles to accommodate us for the trip to the jail. We were placed under arrest but refused to walk to jail so they decided to let us go.

The manager of the restaurant had called the fire department for aid. No trucks showed up but he did have an extinguisher on hand which he never used. I was scared to death because the extinguisher was right behind me. For a while I thought they were going to use it.

We then proceeded to the movie houses from the restaurants. The spirit of the crowd was terrific; we were singing and clapping, having a wonderful time. Finally the movies closed down.

Last night as a result of the concentrated picketing McDonald's agreed to integrate its three stores in Greensboro. The kids were shouting all over the campus about this achievement. I hope this spirit keeps up, because there are quite a number who are ready to go to jail without bail. We'll lick'em, sooner or later. They'll have to open up all facilities soon! You can see I'm pretty excited.

The City Council meets first thing in the morning. We'll plan our next action after we hear what's what.

I guess this is it. Love to everyone...

Saturday, May 18, 1963
Dear folks
A demonstration was called for 2 0'clock this afternoon. We met and the kids were taken up into two groups — those who were willing to be jailed and those who just wanted to picket. Well I decided to go to jail.
I haven't seen a newspaper, but there must have been about 300 or 400 kids who said they would be willing to be

jailed. We met in a church because the city would not allow the Negro YMCA to let CORE hold any more meetings there. Before going downtown we sang songs. The spirit was terrific. Finally we filed downtown and were arrested. I was arrested on a charge of obstructing a fire exit, which I wasn't but later the charge was changed to "trespassing." Since the city has arrested about 600 people in the last couple of days there was no more room for anyone in the City jail....I was sent to a county home which had once been used for polio....

When I arrived no one seemed to know what was going on. Finally we were sent to a room where we had to wait to be fingerprinted. This took a few hours (4). If we wanted to go for water or to the bathroom a policeman escorted us. (Most of them this far seem to be pretty nice) The captain was nasty but that's to be expected. I was finger printed and mugged. I am number 59611. I was tickled because on the record card there was a place for "complexion" of the individual. The officer who was writing the report checked me as fair. I didn't know he knew the difference.

We were arrested about 4:30 PM and didn't eat until about 9:00. We were all starving. People in the city made us sandwiches to eat. (I understand that those under arrest are guaranteed only one meal a day). In the interim of waiting for food a boy pretended that he was ill and fainted. When an ambulance was summoned there was nothing wrong with him.

Beds were brought in finally. It certainly is one big mess. There are 7 or 8 girls in two beds pushed together. Well, this is about it for the evening. I've had an interesting day. Will write tomorrow. Good night.

P.S. I just received my warrant. I'm under $100.00 bond.

Sunday, May 19, 1963

Thus far the morning has been interesting. Sleep last night was almost impossible. We figured it out this morning. There are about 120 girls with about 30 beds. You can imagine there is some confusion. For breakfast we had grits, eggs, (terrible) and some horrid meat. I managed to eat some of it...someone sent newspapers. Cigarettes, toothpaste and brushes to us. Dr. Player came over yesterday to see us. She said she's behind us. We're sending a complaint note to Dr. Player about inadequate facilities... this sheriff had the nerve to state in the newspaper that he had adequate facilities to house 1,000 to 2,000 persons...

The morale of the group is still pretty high. We sing a lot. This helps. This evening has been swell. People are really wonderful. The girls and the fellows at school have been sending us packages with food and clothing. The kids have been writing us letters. About 2,500-3,000 persons have come to protest in front of the "jail". For about two hours they've sung songs and prayed. It's great! I understand that the conditions of the jail are being exposed to the public. Letters and telegrams are being sent to Robert and John Kennedy and others. I understand the fire department was asked to come out and inspect the premises but they never showed up. The sanitation dep't was out here and on the outside....I forgot to tell you the police had dogs outside yesterday for the people in front of the jail. If they use them, Greensboro will be integrated immediately, I'm sure....

The fellows gave us a talent show. We watched from across the hall. I understand that the kids were making jokes about the Whites in Mississippi. The cops got mad and told us to return to our room. We did but made so much noise that they had to let the talent show continue....

That is all for now- Write soon. Love, Phillis

cↄ•◇ cↄ•◇ cↄ•◇ cↄ•◇

Monday May 20, 1963
Dear folks,
Kids are still coming — it's like one big reunion There is
more noise and rejoicing. The police will probably start
getting nasty since there are so many of us here. Bennett
students have 100% backing from the faculty. I read some
of Gibran's words. I've become better acquainted with
some of the girls I've known since freshman year. It's a
shame that it took so long...lunch was terrible. I ate
peaches and milk. Spam and beans were also served. For
dinner we had chicken, dried up French fries. Luckily I
have a cold and can't taste a thing.
Monday evening: Dowdy has asked the students of A&T
to come out of jail. So far the girls say they are not leaving.
Sanford is trying to pressure Dowdy and Dowdy is
scared...if the kids leave our purpose will be defeated.
We've come so far — sometimes I don't understand our so-
called leaders....
PS: I want you to know it is 2:00AM in the morning and
all this foolishness is going on here....It is so crowded that
some of the fellows were moved to the armory. They sent a
message back that they were sleeping on a damp and mist
floor, but they were staying tight and they want us to do
the same.
The new kids that came in tonight have no place to sleep so
we gave them our sheets and mattresses. The spirit of the
group is terrific. It really is a moving experience. I only
wish you could hear us sing "Hold On" and "I've Got
Freedom On My Mind" and "We Shall Not Be Moved"
It's almost all over for Greensboro.
The ministers have ordered a boycott of the town's
shopping areas. Someone is planning a massive march on

town of several thousands of adults on Wednesday night. Will write more in the morning....

Wednesday, May 21
Well, my dear family, I really don't know where to begin.... I can't say that I hate Whites because I know I would be lying But I'll tell you the truth... I was pretty disgusted this evening. It all started last night as I told you before when Dowdy told the A&T students to leave and they refused. We were getting ready for bed when a message was sent to the students that they had to leave. If they didn't leave peacefully they would be removed bodily....there was sheer chaos. The fellows came from their room and climbed through the windows into the room we were in. No one seemed to know what was going on. Some said go- some said stay, some said practice civil disobedience. Picture a room with about 200 people in it standing on beds screaming and hollering. The girls from Bennett were in tears, the A&T girls were crying because we felt that if the other students left the cause would be lost when everyone was behind us. The fellows were trying to comfort us. Two girls went into hysterics while the cops stood around gaping. One cop cursed and wanted to know what kind of people we were, because he said there was a girl dying and if she did we would be responsible ...I got mad and had to call him a couple of names...Finally the boys decided to practice civil disobedience. The cops started dragging the boys out....At about 1:30 AM everyone from A&T had left....Dr. Player isn't going to insist upon our leaving....We drafted a letter of thanks to the President and the student body for their support....
Good morning, more later.

Wednesday night May 21, 1963
Dear folk
About 11:00 Dr. Player came to see us. And explained what had transpired in our absence. All kinds of committees had been set up to keep communications between us and the outside world. Dr. Player told us not to worry about our finals; she said we would have ample time to make up our work. The seniors who met requirements for graduation would graduate regardless...She also said no one was going to pressure her into doing anything she did not want to do. This made us feel better.

After the meeting with Miss Player we had a meeting with one of CORE'S lawyers. The lawyer felt it would help his legal strategy if we would consent to leave jail for a couple of hours. He explained that then he could tell the mayor that he had approximately five hours to do something about the situation because at 5 o'clock that evening a mass demonstration was being planned. We voted to leave...When I got to the campus all the kids were waiting for us. Guess what I did immediately? I took a BATH...I hadn't had one in five days. I ate dinner and packed my clothes for another tenure....

Thursday May 22, 1963I understand that the committee didn't accomplish anything so tonight we have no alternative except to go to jail...I understand that the cops are not going to keep anyone in jail....Something has to happen soon...

(Letter written on May 28)

Wed. we were released...A few of us tried to enter other establishments such as hotels. I was sent to the King Cotton Hotel where the manager told us that we did not have reservations...we were finally arrested for 'loitering and blocking a public entrance. All told 15 kids arrested. We were booked and released that evening. The patrolman who drove us home was pretty nice. He told us that Gov. Sanford had issued some type of ordinance stating that all students arrested had to be released because the city was unable to feed and house us adequately.

Friday evening there was a kneel-in and prayer service at the courthouse. That evening my roommate and 8 other students decided to stage a Sit-in at the mayor's office. They were prepared to spend the week-end but the police had to remove them bodily from the office. The kids were placed in chairs and carried out to the jail. They too were released.

A truce was called over the week-end. Presently nothing has happened. Committees are still meeting but no definite action has taken place.... Miss Player told roommate that we should pack and prepare to leave on June 3rd...Miss Player also added that if she could help it there would be no more trials....I think this is about it for now. Finals have started but not too many people seem affected. Thanks for everything, Love, Phillis

Terry, Esther Alexander '61 (Interview in person, October 31, 2011)

I had been something of a community "activist" in my home town of Wise, North Carolina well before I entered Bennett College. Early on I had gained special stature in the eyes of the older men and women in my neighborhood as a child who could be trusted to perform certain deeds that ranged from dispensing their medicines to paying their bills. After farmers were granted the right to social security in 1957, I became quite efficient at searching out documents that would provide proof of age for the men in my community who had no birth certificates. In a word I accepted and I lived out the community's characterization of me as a "good girl," and I understood all of these activities as being "character building"--- laying the foundation for a responsible, safe adulthood, largely within the confines of the existing system of American apartheid. Attending college would be the final step in my preparation for that life.

Providently, at Bennett I came under the influence of a faculty committed to providing us with an education that would make us dissatisfied with second-class citizenship. They were adamant in their belief that it was folly to aspire to leadership positions on the campus while accepting anything less than full citizenship outside the campus walls. Dr. Rose Karfiol who had brought with her the experience of Nazi Germany, for example, and Drs. Hobart Jarrett, John Hatchett, and Edward Edmonds, who had long histories of fighting injustice on American soil (to name but a few) infused such a distain for injustice into their teaching that what we learned from them, and consequently, about our history and ourselves, laid the foundation for our participation in the Sit-ins. It was at Bennett that I became inculcated with the philosophy that if my education were to be meaningful, I would be required to do more than merely help others (or even myself) live their lives within the world as it existed. Bennett taught me that a meaningful education came with a responsibility not only to recognize injustice, but to act against it.

My parents were conflicted about my participation in the Sit-ins. Like all of our parents they wanted their children to be safe, but at the same time they understood the importance and inevitability of what we were doing. At the beginning I settled for their reluctant endorsement. As for us students, we were not cavalier about what lay before us; we knew we were going into danger. Yet we were prepared to go forth—as the only way to a full, uncompromised citizenship. We had been the beneficiaries of the encouragement and examples provided by the likes of Dr. Martin Luther King, Dr. Benjamin Mays, and so many others who had appeared before us as speakers in our chapel. We had the example and support of our president, Dr. Willa B. Player, and the guidance of the faculty. And ultimately, despite their fears, I had the unqualified support of my parents who knew in their hearts that the battle we were fighting was but a continuation of the war against injustice that they had been fighting even as they had sought to keep me safe. They like so many of our parents, came to accept that in this war for equality there was no safety.

And finally we had each other. I don't believe that we could have done what we did without the bond of sisterhood that had been developed among us at the college. Once we were at the Sit-ins we had strict organizational rules that were designed to keep us focused and on point as we navigated through the crowds of hecklers and on-lookers. And though that structure brought some feelings of security, for me, it was the fact of our sisterhood that provided that extra layer of courage that outweighed any fear that might have overwhelmed me. I sat next to Linda Brown at the Woolworth counter. She and I went downtown together on February 3 in a car with some other classmates. I remember that we were quiet on the short ride. While we might have felt some fear and anxiety, we were not conflicted in the least about our actions. We knew what we were supposed to do. We were taking responsible action to make the nation live up to its promise. We were together in this activism that we knew had to be part of a meaningful education. That's what we had been taught at Bennett. As graduates we still hear that drumbeat even now over 50 years later.

It was an enormous thing, this preparation for leadership that we received at Bennett; and I want this book to celebrate the

College, its early founders and their philosophy, its remarkable leadership, especially that of Dr. Willa B. Player, its exceptional faculty, and my Bennett sisters for the role they played in helping to change our nation. I am so fortunate to have been educated at Bennett. It was and continues to be, in the words of Dr. David Dallas Jones, "a small but important college."

Walker, Sonia Louden '58

I organized with peers to seek a teen center in Yellow Springs, Ohio in 1953-54. I graduated before the Sit-ins began but I was one of those at Bennett with Deloris Tonkins Dozier who tried to initiate a boycott of the Carolina Theater. I actually initiated the "Let's do something conversation" after viewing the film about the bus boycott in Montgomery.

Warren, Geraldine Kearney '66

I first engaged in social activism at Bennett. Dr. Martin Luther King and the news motivated me. I participated in the silent marching downtown. This activity taught me patience and perseverance in dealing with challenges. My experience was minimal but very influential.

Washington, Emma Howie '62

I was a social activist at birth and have been a social activist all my life. I was born a Black girl in the South and activism was a daily given; you went up the back stairs of department stores or you chose not to shop in that store, ate from the back window of a bus so you could pack a lunch when you were traveling and many other inequalities. So...a lifetime of activism. I had followed the Civil Rights Movement as long as I could remember, so when I went to Bennett things were already buzzing. I heard Dr. King was coming to Greensboro and I wondered if I would be able to see him and as it turned out our President Dr. Willa B. Player would be the only one in Greensboro to give him a venue to speak! It was then I knew we

(Bennett women) were going to be a part of something that would change my life.

Under a great and very competent Dr. Player we became involved in a great and very important movement. I sat-in and picketed. My greatest impression was the spiritual emotional and educational leadership we received from our faculty members, especially Dr. Player who would gather us in the chapel every morning for an inspirational talk and prayer. As I remember all our faulty members were positive and supportive. My participation in the Sit-ins had a profound influence on my life.

During our Easter break of 1960 I took two of my Bennett friends home. One was a White exchange student who had decided to stay and graduate from Bennett. The other friend was Black. My parents were very reluctant to have my White girlfriend in the house lest we all be the recipient of reprisals from the White people of Concord NC where I was from. As a result we stayed with a former high school mentor of mine for the weekend in Concord. I was not unaware that this was considered "dangerous." I now know that was part of my rebellion against racism, and part of my activist mentality. I became a Black woman born in the South knowing that I was now armed with the tools to overcome any inequalities with which I was going to be faced at any point in my life. I was "Young Gifted and Black" and now I am "Older Gifted and Black."

Watkins, Opal Hughes '63

Jessie Jackson was usually the speaker when I attended the rallies....Mr. James Farmer spoke at a number of the rallies...Both influenced my life and my thinking about race, injustices, being proud to be a "Negro,"" Colored," at that time.

Williams-Thomas, Johnsie '61

When I was in high school, I helped with voter registration in Eden, NC. My father was an activist and transported his neighbors, friends and others to the polls. I do not remember who did the training in non-violence but we were advised. We would remain focused, not retaliate, and keep moving in the lines. I was never arrested, but my sister was at Shaw University and she was jailed in Raleigh. My parents were always supportive of the demonstrations. The Bennett faculty and administrators were very supportive of the movement. I remember the cross that was burned in front of Dr. Player's home.The demonstrations enhanced my life. I still remember the speech that Dr. King gave on our campus.

Wilson, Karen Leach '61

My father came one week-end and he said, "Sugar I did not send you to college to fight White people! I subcontract with them and they are helping to send you to school! "My response was, Daddy some White people are good but we are fighting against the ones who are not! I also told my daddy that those of us who rode the bus and train integrated the bus and train stations in Greensboro during my freshman year! There were too many of us to sit in the "colored side"; the authorities never tried to remove us. My Dad finally said, "OK Sugar just be careful and don't go to jail. I want you to graduate on time. I want you to come home and teach." I did. That was the end of our ever discussing the subject again. [Please see the page 78 for Karen Leach's letter to the editor published Feb 1960 by the *Greensboro Daily News*] .

Later, I became the most defiant faculty member in my school because I spoke up when I witnessed any injustice in regard to faculty and students. As a result the entire school schedule was changed because a White principal gave all the Black teachers 'Average'.

Bennett Belles Honor Roll

The names listed here consist of Bennett students who participated in the effort to desegregate Greensboro, North Carolina from 1960 to 1963. There may be missing names, as it was not possible to gather a completely accurate list fifty years later. As we honor the names below, we also honor and remember all those whose names have been lost to history.

Albea, Hermine (Bacote) '63
Almada. Mettoe (Crawford)'62
Bell, Gwendolyn '60
Bender, Mary Ellen '60
Bennett, Edna (Jackson) '59
Blake, Doris (Neely) '61
Blair, Gloria Jean (Howard) '64
Bolton, Marion '59
*Brooks, Carolyn (Snead) '63
*Breown, Gloria '60
Brown, Linda Beatrice '61
Byron-Twyman, Freda K.
        Thompson '66
Carpenter, Regina
Carson, Diane (Mitchell) '64
Cheagle, Roslyn '62
Clark, Anthanette (Thomas) '65
Dixon, Faye (McClain) '66
Dorcas, Carolyn (Brown) '58
Dozier, Deloris (Tonkins) '58
Dusenbury, Jacqueline
        (Florance) '62
Edmonds, Gloria (Gilchrist) '64
Evans, Joyce Y. '64
Faison, Charlotte Marie (Tenbrook) '66
Faulkner, Betty '60
(Finger)-Wright, Dolores '61
Garner, Marilyn (Frazier) '60
Grafton, Nannie (Hughes) '59
Graham, Shirley (Dismuke) '61
Gunn, Sondra (Steven) '66
Harley, Betty Jo '61
Gunn, Sondra (Steven) '66
Harley, Betty Jo '61

Hawthorne, Willa (Pullens) "60
Herbin, Francis (Lewis)
Huey, Joyce (Phelps) '64
Jackson, Jean (Franklin)
  Michaela '63
Jacobs, Elsie L. '65
Jenkins, Ellarene '66
Jessup, Gladys (Jeffries) '59
Johnson, Jewel (Merritt) '66
Johnson, Ollie '62
Johnson, Yvonne (Jeffries) '64
Jones, Barbara (Jackson) '62
Jones, Sarah Outterbridge
Kearney, Geraldine (Warren) '66
Kersey, VonDeleath (Moore) '61
Kirby, Nancy '60
Mackel, Marilyn '65
Matthew, Claraleata (Cutter) '64
(McAllister)-Harper, Desretta '62
McBride, Sandra '61
*McCain, Bettye (Davis) '63
McFarland, Shirley (Johnson) '58
McKie, Carolyn (Maddox) '66
Mims, Judith (Jones) '66
Moore, Shirley '58
Morton, Iris (Jeffries) '61
Murray, Patricia
Neff, Jean (Herbert) (exchange
  student, 1959/60)
Nevell, Juanita '59
Nims, Gloria (Lee) '63
Powell, Susie '64
Pyatt, Gwendolyn '59

Bennett Belles Honor Roll

The names listed here consist of Bennett students who participated in the effort to desegregate Greensboro, North Carolina from 1960 to 1963. There may be missing names, as it was not possible to gather a completely accurate list fifty years later. As we honor the names below, we also honor and remember all those whose names have been lost to history.

Revell, Yvonne (Lyons) '60
Rice, Gwendolyn (Mackel) '61
Riggs, Elizabeth A. '63
Roberts, Doris (Alston) '64
Ryder, Jane A. '65
Satterfield, Shirley Ann '63
Sharpe, Sandra (Echols) '65
Sizemore, Dorinda (Smith) '66
Smith, Hazel Elizabeth (Abron) '63
Smith, Roslyn '61
Soublet, Beatrice (Perry) Stanley '65
Stokes, Alma '64
Taylor, Phillis (Strong) '64
Terry, Esther (Alexander) '61
Urquhart, Margaret (Bailey) '61
Walker, Sonia (Louden) '58
Warren, Geraldine (Kearney) '66
Washington, Emma (Howie) '62
Watkins, Opal (Hughes) '63
William-(Thomas), Johnsie '61
Williams, Brenda (Walker) '66
*Williams, Lois (Lucas) '64
Wilson, Betty Jo Foster '65
Wilson, Karen (Leach) '61

*Deceased

Bennett College Faculty and Staff

*Breathett, George
Corry, John
*Edmonds, Edward
*Hatchett, John
*Jarrett, Hobart
*Laizner, Elizabeth
McMillan, James
*Player, Willa Beatrice
Stanley, Anthony

*Deceased

வேஜேஜேஜேஜே

Afterword

Daughters of Harriet

The iconic Harriet Tubman stands as the first great named African American heroine. She taught us by example that one person could change the world. More to the point, she taught us that one lone Black woman with faith and courage and gumption could change the world. Gender was for Tubman a total irrelevance, in a time when the cult of true womanhood reigned over the White Western world. She is for Black Americans what Jeanne D'Arc is for France, standing outside of history, our eternal Black woman. Full of the Light of what she knew as God's truth, she acted always on that truth. We are her daughters.

How can we be so arrogant as to declare that we are the daughters of Harriet Tubman, the greatest Black woman activist in the history of the United States? I use this word daughter out of reverence for what Harriet Tubman represents. We are the children of her legacy, the inheritors of this great life of sacrifice.

There are many ways in which we can see the Bennett history connected to the legacy of her life. The deep faith of Tubman resonates throughout her life. Bennett College was founded out of the faith of those Methodist women who saw its potential for the liberation of its students. Although the

Methodist Church had a checkered relationship to the Civil Rights Movement, the connection of the College to its faith-based history has never been severed. The convictions of Presidents Jones and Player and their understanding of the mission of Christian higher education is fully documented in their words and their actions.

Seen in the context of the Civil Rights Movement, Bennett College is the most American of Colleges. It begins as a statement of liberty and justice for all, declaring its relationship to freedom of the oppressed. Bennett came into a world that was birthing itself anew. America was not ten years out of its most horrendous conflict when the emancipated African Americans decided that education was such a priority that they had to act and they began a school in Greensboro, one of many such schools throughout the South. To this affirmation of the value of education, was added the affirmation that Black Americans are equal to all other Americans and deserving of the blessings of a free country. Our calling was to become the best that we could become. The calling was to education, to live up to our God given potential, and to do this not for selfish reasons but for the benefit of all. Such a calling echoes Harriet Tubman's words: "I did not take up this work for my own benefit but for those of my race who need help. The work is now well started and I know God will raise up others to take care of the future."

The activism of the Bennett women happened because it was the logical outgrowth of an authentic liberal education with its commitment to democratic principals. But more, there is a seamless tapestry of liberation, education, democracy, and spirituality that existed in the creation of this College and still stands. Throughout the civil rights period, the leadership of the College makes reference to democracy and its mandates. It would not have made sense for Bennett and her students to ignore the growing call for freedom that was sweeping the country; rather it would have been unthinkable for a Bennett College to have done anything else.

Finally, what can we claim was the result of this extraordinary effort to change a city, and ultimately to change a country, by these young women of courage and their institution, whose mission was so much more than academic training? Bennett College had taken up this high calling, perhaps some may say it was a calling beyond the reach of any institution— to attempt to reform the culture of a hide-bound small Southern town, and so have an effect on the country at large.

A great deal has been written about the impact and success or failure of the Civil Rights Movement. Certainly there are results that are obvious to all of us. The segregating laws are gone. Customs and practices that had been in place were wiped away. On many fronts the lives of African Americans were changed for the better. The fall-out from that national sea change is still going on, and as a city, Greensboro more or less followed the national trends.

One major result of the activism of the Bennett students must be its impact on the lives of the activists themselves. One question sent to the alumnae was: How did your participation in the 60's movement influence the rest of your life? There is no way to read the responses of these women without being struck by their commitment to making a contribution to racial justice in America. In a great variety of ways these women continued after graduation to be change agents. In their narratives they document specific activities of their post graduate lives and in some cases they include comments on the growth of personal strength, courage and risk taking that was the result of their having been part of the Greensboro movement. Their narratives include evidence of personal transformation, which must of necessity be part of an attempt to transform the world. It is clear that the Bennett women quoted here were further liberated by their attempts to liberate. They learned that without a doubt they were free within, in spite of the segregated and oppressive "rules" and attitudes of racist America. Harriet Tubman declared she freed thousands of slaves. But then she added, "I could have freed more, if they had known they were slaves." We know from our understanding of the Bennett history that owning one's power was a lesson taught from the origins of the College. The activities of 1958 to 1963 were a graphic and kinesthetic lesson in personal and collective liberation.

That these women had children who have inherited their view of responsibility to make the world a better place may go without saying, but of course this is not a measurable result. Neither do we have any way of knowing how effective their on-the-job activism was, although some of them indicate success in their narratives. In many cases they went on to participate in other civil rights demonstrations and to become engaged in community efforts to bring justice where there was obvious injustice. Large numbers of the respondents indicated that Greensboro was a training ground for them. Significant numbers of them indicate that the Greensboro experience was a life changing experience.

Passing the torch of liberation to the next generation is more and more a necessity. Our polarized world must find its hope for reconciliation in the great granddaughters of Harriet Tubman. This legacy that stretches back for almost 200 years must be passed on. My hope is that this story of the stand taken by the Belles of Liberty and their College will bring growing awareness to the young people of today, for there is still a great work ahead, perhaps more complicated than ever, "to proclaim liberty to the captives and the opening of the prison to them that are bound."

Appendix

The documents that follow support and illustrate an overview of the scope and significance of the role played by Bennett College from the years 1958 to 1963, an extraordinarily important period in the struggle for civil rights in Greensboro, North Carolina. Most are copies of rare, original historical documents and photographs and show the wear of fifty years of various private and public archives.

APPENDIX CONTENTS

APPENDIX I
BENNETT MATERIALS

Telegram Sent by Willa Player to the Parents of Incarcerated Students

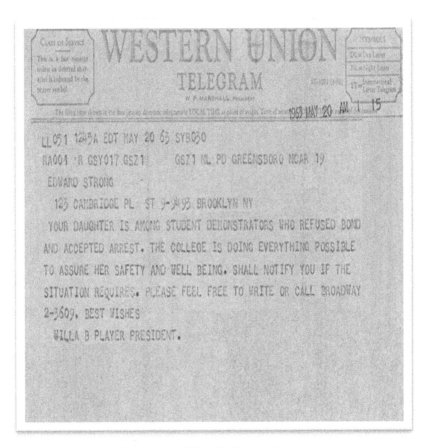

Courtesy of Phyllis Strong Taylor
Bennett College Class of 1964

NAACP Presents Martin Luther King

The Greensboro Branch

of the

National Association for the

Advancement of Colored People

Presents

Dr. Martin Luther King, Jr.

THE ANNIE MERNER PFEIFFER CHAPEL

Bennett College

Greensboro, North Carolina

FEBRUARY 11, 1958

at 8:00 p. m.

Program

Presiding, DR. EDWIN R. EDMONDS

President, Greensboro Branch

HYMN, NUMBER 491: "America"
(The audience will please stand to sing the Hymns.)
Mr. Clarence E. Whiteman, *Organist*

SCRIPTURE AND PRAYER..........................Reverend Julius T. Douglas
Pastor, St. James Presbyterian Church

MUSIC...The Greensboro Men's Glee Club
Mrs. E. Logan Penn, *Director*

LIFTING OF THE OFFERING.........................Mr. N. L. Gregg
Treasurer, North Carolina State Conference of Branches

MUSIC...The Greensboro Men's Glee Club

INTRODUCTION OF THE SPEAKER.............Reverend C. W. Anderson
Pastor, United Institutional Baptist Church

THE ADDRESS............................Dr. Martin Luther King, Jr.
Montgomery, Alabama

HYMN, NUMBER 507: "In Christ There Is No East or West"

BENEDICTION.............................Reverend G. M. Phelps
Pastor, Union Memorial Methodist Church

CONTRIBUTORS TO THE GREENSBORO APPEARANCE OF
OF DR. MARTIN LUTHER KING, JR.

Mrs. Bessie Griffin
Mrs. W. M. Grimes
Mr. and Mrs. Melvin H. Groomes
Mr. J. H. Hagins
Mrs. Georgia Haith
Mrs. Ruth S. Haith
Mr. and Mrs. F. J. Hardy
Reverend and Mrs. F. A. Hargett
Mrs. Lucy Hargrove
Mr. Estell Harper
Mr. John D. Harrell
Mr. C. T. Harris
Mr. E. O. Harris
Miss Cecile Harrison
Mr. W. B. Harrison, Sr.
Mr. Preston Haygood
Mrs. Margaret Headen
Mr. William H. Headen
Mr. Frank Henderson
Mr. and Mrs. J. D. Henry
Mr. and Mrs. Charles Herbin
Miss R. Winifred Heyward
Atty. and Mrs. Major S. High
Mr. David Hinton
Mrs. Annie D. Holder
Mrs. Lancelot Holder
Mr. LeRoy Holmes
Miss Pearl Holt
Mr. Jesse Hopkins
Mr. E. C. Horne
Mrs. Lillian Houston
Mr. and Mrs. C. O. Howell
Mr. and Mrs. Dorse Howell
Dr. and Mrs. George Hunter
Mr. and Mrs. J. C. Hunter
Mrs. Mabel Hutchinson
Mr. Clark H. Ireland
Mr. J. C. Ireland
Miss Florine Irvin
Dr. Arthur M. Jackson
Mrs. Betty C. James
Dr. and Mrs. Hobart Jarrett
Dr. and Mrs. J. E. Jeffries
Mr. J. W. Jeffries
Dr. and Mrs. W. M. Jenkins
Mr. Ralph Johns
Mrs. Bertha J. Johnson
Miss Loretta Johnson
Mrs. Lucile Johnson
Mr. Malcolm Johnson
SFC Norris Johnson
Mr. S. A. Johnson
Mr. S. L. Johnson
Miss Vivian K. Johnson
Reverend W. D. Johnson
Mr. Arthur C. Jones
Mrs. David D. Jones
Dr. N. N. Jones
Mr. R. E. Jones, Jr.
Mr. Robert L. Jones
Mr. Sebron Jones
Mr. Wendell P. Jones
Captain and Mrs. William L. Jones
Mrs. Wilson Jones
Mr. Cleo Jordan
Dr. Rose Karfiol
Mrs. Carrye H. Kelley
Dr. W. L. Kennedy
Mrs. A. B. Kitchen
Mrs. C. Brown Lamb
Mr. Daniel Lanier
Miss Wilhelmina R. Laws
Miss L. L. Leath
Reverend P. L. Ledbetter
Mr. and Mrs. Arthur Lee, Jr.
Mrs. Bernice LeGette
Atty. and Mrs. J. Kenneth Lee
Mrs. Virginia Lee

Mr. and Mrs. Matthew Lewis
Mrs. Dorothy Lightfoot
Mrs. Hardy Liston, Jr.
Dr. and Mrs. Perry P. Little
Dr. and Mrs. F. A. Logan
Mr. Edward Lowe
Mr. W. T. McAllister
Miss Maxine McBrier
Mr. Vernable McCloud
Reverend Cleo M. McCoy
Mr. John McCoy
Mr. David K. McDowell
Miss Burdette McIver
Mr. G. B. McNair
Mrs. R. E. McNair
Dr. W. O. McNair
Mr. Charles McLean
Mr. and Mrs. J. C. McMillan
Mr. Clarkie McMillian
Mrs. Evelyn D Mainer
Mr. and Mrs. William P. Malone
Mrs. Nan Manuel
Mrs. Loreno M. Marrow
Mr. Nat Marshburn
Mr. Milton Martin
Mrs. Angelita Maynard
Mr. and Mrs. C. C. Miller
Mr. Daniel E. Miller
Mr. J. F. Miller
Dr. and Mrs. W. L. T. Miller
MILTON'S ESSO SERVICE
STATION
Mrs. Gladys H. Minor
Mrs. Geraidine Mitchell
Mrs. Norman Mitchell
Mr. Norman Moon
Mrs. A. B. Moore
Miss Amaleta Moore
Mrs. Anne B. Moore
Mr. R. H. Moore
Mr. and Mrs. Winston Moore, Jr.
Mr. and Mrs. D. W. Morehead
Mr. Dorsey Morgan
Mr. J. E. Morgan
Mr. and Mrs. Allen Morrison
Captain and Mrs. John W. Mosley
Mr. and Mrs. W. R. Mueller
Mrs. B. B. Murchison
Mr. Samuel Murray
Mr. Wm. H. Neal
Mr. and Mrs. M. L. Neely
Mr. and Mrs. W. N. Nelson
Mrs. Myrtle Nesbitt
Mr. Ernest Nettles, Jr.
Mr. J. H. Nicholson
Mr. Timothy Norman
Mrs. O. B. Norris
Mrs. Florence Norwood
Mr. John D. Parks
Mr. John W. Patterson
Mr. and Mrs. D. E. Paylor
Mr. Howard T. Pearsall
Mr. and Mrs. M. H. Peek
Mrs. Jane Penley
Mrs. Norma Pennix
Mr. Charles F. Perry
Mr. and Mrs. J. W. Pettiford
Reverend and Mrs. G. M. Phelps
PHI BETA SIGMA FRATERNITY,
Gamma Beta Sigma Chapter
Mr. George Phillips
Mr. and Mrs. George O. Phillips
Dr. Willa B. Player
Miss Marguerite Porter
Miss Toni Presley
Mr. I. J. Prince
Mrs. E. L. Raiford

Mr. Ang Ray
Mr. Isaac Reid
Mrs. James H. Reid
Mrs. L. E Reynolds, Sr.
Mr. Lonnie Reynolds, Jr.
REYNOLDS BARBER SHOP
Mr. and Mrs. Lewis Richards
Mr. Armand Richardson
Mr. John Richmond
Sgt. Willie Riles
Mrs. George M. Roberts
Mr. and Mrs. H. S. Robinson, Jr.
Dr. and Mrs. L. H. Robinson
Mr. William H. Robinson
Mr. Robert L. Rogers
Dr. and Mrs. George Royal
Reverend W. R. Royster
Mr. Charles Sanders
Mrs. Thelma Sandifer
Dr. J. Henry Sayles
Mr. and Mrs. J. J. Scarlette
Mr. and Mrs. Alfred Scott
Mr. Nathan T. Seely
Mrs. Lillian B. Shaw
Mr. Samuel J. Shaw
Mrs. Beulah Shoffner
Mr. P. P. Shoffner
Dr. and Mrs. G. C. Simkins, Jr.
Dr. and Mrs. G. C. Simkins, Sr.
Mrs. S. B. Simmons
Mrs. Lucy T. Sligh
Mr. Harold Smith
Mrs. Mary D. Smith
Mr. P. M. Smith
Mr. and Mrs. Clifton T. Snipes
Mr. and Mrs. J. A. Spaulding
Mr. William Spruiel
Miss Serena Staggers
Mr. J. M. R. Stevenson
Mr. and Mrs. W. A. Streat
Dr. and Mrs. Virgil C. Stroud
Dr. and Mrs. J. L. Stuart
Mr. Joseph Sturdivant
Mrs. Juanita Tate
Mr. Harold Taylor
Mr. L. S. Taylor
Mr Robert Luther Taylor
Mr. and Mrs. Everett Thomas
Mrs. Marian Thomas
Dr. and Mrs. Eulyss Troxler
Mr. Herman Turner
Captain and Mrs. Leonard F. Turner
Mrs. J. A. Viverette, Jr.
Mrs. Gary Voss
Mr. Leonard Wadlington
Mrs. Emma Wallace
Mrs. Ruth Warren
Mr. Alexander W. Washington
SFC Allison M. Webb, Jr.
Bishop and Mrs. Wyoming Wells
Mr. Clarence E. Whiteman
Mrs. Lola Ann Whitfield
Miss Naomi Whiting
Mrs. Ida Bell Wilkins
Mr. Baxter Williams
Mr. James A. Williams
Reverend F. Stoney Williams
Mrs. Ivy B. Williamson
Reverend and Mrs. R. W. Winchester
Dr. Chauncey G. Winston
Mr. L. A. Wise
Mr. C. R. Wyrick
Mr. and Mrs. Willie L. Young
YOUR BARBER SHOP
Mrs. M. R. Zachary
Mrs. Marta Zalitis
AND FRIENDS

Operation Door Knock Booklet

then someone remembered that 1960, throughout the length and breadth of the nation, would be an election year.

As the idea was tossed back and forth, enthusiasm began to mount. Getting people interested in politics was a good idea but how could this best be done? As any politician knows, getting people to vote is important but before this can be done, they must be registered. Why not, the committee thought, stage a sort of blitz campaign to get more registered voters on the books?

At first, it was felt that the Bennett students might undertake the task of covering the entire city with their effort, but the realization that there would be only three nights in which to accomplish this feat made it apparent that the task would be too enormous for this limited time.

It was then suggested that the registration drive be limited to the precinct in which the college is located—Precinct No. 7. A quick study of the political map revealed that this precinct covered an area of 1.04 square miles, with a population of approximately 2,700 persons of voting age.

President Willa B. Player, herself a member of the planning committee, was enthusiastic about the great potential of such an intensive campaign and while a theme or slogan was not immediately forthcoming, it was agreed unanimously that the project would be undertaken.

Because all committees at the college have student representations, it was decided that these members might sound out their "sisters" in a sort of "trial balloon" fashion to get their reactions to the proposal. The results were more than enough to convince the committee that this was "IT."

A headquarters office was set up on the second floor of the David D. Jones Student Union. Student volunteers manned the office throughout the day. From the Board of Elections cards were obtained containing the names of all registered voters in the precinct. The unregistered voters were then determined by checking these cards against the city directory. These lists were then duplicated in quantity.

Mrs. Vivian C. Mason gives pointers to student leaders

A huge street map of the precinct was made showing the location of the homes of all non-registered persons and the streets were then divided by "odd" and "even" side designations, so that students assigned to any given block would be required to work only one side of the street, thereby saving considerable time.

To give direction to the project, it was decided to call in two persons with wide experience in the voter registration field. Mrs. Vivian Carter Mason, of Norfolk, Va., and Russell B. Sugarmon, Jr., Memphis, Tenn., attorney, were called in for inspirational meetings with the entire student body and later with the volunteer leaders from the campus and community.

The stimulation from their visits was almost miraculous and Mrs. Constance H. Marteena, college librarian, prepared and distributed an extensive bibliography giving listings of books, films, recordings and other materials which the students might use in preparing themselves for the task ahead. The NAACP and the AFL-CIO Committee on Political Education were most co-operative in providing voting materials for free distribution.

As the program began to take form, the theme: "Register and Vote! A Necessity for Good Citizenship" was adopted and to dramatize the campaign, the designation "Operation Doorknock" was given. Materials were sent to the public schools and churches, and handbills, giving a brief announcement of the campaign, flooded the area. It was impossible for anyone to be alive and not to know about the Bennett project because the daily newspapers, radio and TV stations— sensing the newsworthiness of it. began to repeat the story.

To set the stage for "Operation Doorknock" the committee was fortunate to obtain Thurgood Marshall, of New York City, chief legal counsel for the NAACP, as its "kickoff" speaker, and Dr. Benjamin E. Mays, of Atlanta, Georgia, president of Morehouse College, as its closing speaker.

Said President Player in her statément of introduction in the printed program: "The theme . . . is seen by Bennett College as significantly related to our responsibility to help our students and our community to be alive to the cross currents of change and the part we must play in bringing constructive change to pass. This is inherent in a people's search for freedom."

There was standing room only on Sunday, April 3. for the Marshall address, in which the noted lawyer said, among other things:

"Stop wringing your hands and condemning everybody and start doing something. Don't wait for someone to tell you what to do. See what needs to be done and do it!"

The next day, John M. Brooks, of Richmond. Va., director of voter registration for the NAACP, continued in this vein with a demonstration-lecture on registration techniques in which he reminded the students that there would be nothing glamorous about the task they were undertaking. He warned them of certain types of non-cooperative individuals they would encounter but gave them a set of tested approaches which should offset any apathy, reluctance or opposition.

On this same program, the Lincoln Junior High School Chorus, directed by Mrs. Margaret B. Gill, a Bennett graduate. sang prophetically. "Walk Together Children, Don't You Get Weary."

Following Mr. Brooks's presentation. the students divided into six workshop groups in each of which they received registration materials and instruction in how to use them. Students. teachers and community persons served as leaders in the workshops which were also continued on Tuesday.

Registration materials included qualifications for registration. a copy of the registration oath. a simple introductory statement of purpose and a set of "standard arguments" for hesitant registrants and brief statements about candidates in national elections and the forthcoming state primary.

J. M. Brooks shows how to do the job

ONE of the most unusual community activities ever initiated by college students took place in Bennett College, Greensboro, North Carolina, this past March.

It was called Operation Door Knock because that was what the activity was. It meant that pairs of students went out into the community around the campus and knocked on doors.

Their question was: "Are you a registered voter?"

The students had reasons why persons should vote. They had cars to take people to the registration center. They "baby-sat" or cooked dinners while mothers went out to register.

In three days one thousand prospective new voters were added to the rolls of the electorate of Greensboro. One thousand men and women took their first step toward articulate citizenship. Young college women learned about the world around them.

OPERATION
DOOR
KNOCK

(*Above*) *The activity Operation Door Knock grew out of discussions at this Home-making Institute held by Bennett College during March, 1960.*

(*Left*) *The neighborhood donated cars for the project.*

(*Right*) *The young woman student explains why voting is a duty.*

Photos on these two pages by BENNETT COLLEGE, Greensboro, N. C.

(Right) When this mother decided to register, the girls stepped in and took care of her baby.

(Left) New registrants waiting their turn.

(Right) At the College, public school children of the community came to sing to the initiators of the Operation Door Knock. Their song was, aptly: "Walk Together, Children—Don't Get Weary."

(Left) And the students did not show weariness as they met on the last night. One thousand registrants! One thousand!

APPENDIX II

The Intercollegiate
Council for Racial Equality

"The Intercollegiate Council for Racial Equality is composed of students from Woman's College, Guilford, A&T and Bennett College It was organized in order to bring about unity between the four college campuses in promoting our movement. The Council was originally started by the A&T and Bennett chapters of the NAACP but later merged with groups from Women's and Guilford colleges. The Council is affiliated with the NAACP and the Greensboro Citizens Association."

Procedures for Picketing

1. There will be a main captain at each theater at all times. If the captain has to leave a co-captain will be selected from the group to be responsible.
2. When approached by a reporter your response should always be 'no comment'.
3. In case of arrests only one person need go, and in most cases it will be the captain; try to refrain from mass arrest.
4. There should be 22 people for every hour to work in the picket lines and 25 for the revolving lines, making a total of 49 people leaving campus every hour.
5. You go downtown for either 1, 2, or 3 hours, depending on the time that you have to spare.
6. When you arrive at the theatres, let the captain or co-captain know you have arrived.
7. The captain will be responsible for transportation, especially in the evening. Absolutely no young lady should walk home by herself or in small groups at night! Every weekday there will be no picketers from either of the two schools, A&T or Bennett from 5-7 o'clock. On Sunday Bennett girls will picket from 6-9 and A&T students will take care of the time from 2-6.

8. Always have $.75 just in case you are admitted into the theater.

9. There should always be a young man on the scene just in case there is trouble.

10. The main duties of the captain will be:
    a. Spokesman for the group
    b. Keep picketers and revolving line in order
    c. Be sure that a policeman is always on the scene
    d. Check students that spaced come and go
    e. At night see that young ladies especially have a ride home.
    f. Keep daily reports to be turned in to Donald Brandon
    g. The captains leaving at 2 and 7 should take posters downtown
    h. If legal matters arise that you cannot deal with, contact Donald Lyons who is on the legal committee.

All cars will be leaving from Graham Hall on the hour

Picketers		Revolving lines	
6 at center		5 at Center	
8 at National		10 at National	
8 at Carolina		10 at Carolina	

Two people should be at each theater to pass out pledge cards."

[Source: Roslyn Smith, and Dolores Finger, Bennett class of 1961; personal papers].

Information Sheet About
Student Incarceration

INFORMATION SHEET

CORE

Greensboro, North Carolina

May 19, 1963

Over 700 students have been incarcerated in a county farm
and an abandoned polio hospital for seeking service at resturants
and entrance into theatres in Greensboro, N. C., on May 17 and 18.
We firmly believe that present conditions are extremely dangerous
to their health and safety. Some have been hospitalized as a
result of inadequate provisions and treatment.

A few observations in regard to the Above:

1. A committee headed by the lawyer representing the students,
   Atty. Major High, and composed of Fr. Richard Hicks, Dr.
   Glenn Rankin, Dr. Louis Dowdy, Dr. J. A. Tarpley, Dr. M. L.
   T. Miller, DDS, Dr. George Evans, MD, Dr. A. V. Bount, Jr.,
   MD, was not permitted to investigate the conditions of
   the youths.

2. The over-whelming majority has not been provided with
   beds. This was confirmed by officals.

3. In a room approximately 50' by 30' there are seven beds
   and 75 students. Most have been without beds for two
   nights.

4. On Sunday, May 19, we were not permitted to deliver food
   and what they were provided with is inadequate.

5. Even parents have not been allowed to visit their sons
   and daughters even though promises had been made that
   they could do so.

6. The Mayor has left town and cannot be reached.

Please register your protests immediately with the following:

1. David Schenck
   Mayor
   Greensboro, N. C.   BR 4-2048

2. W. T. Jackson, Police Captain
   Greensboro Police Department   BR 2-4141

3. Clayton Jones, Sheriff Guilford County
   High Point, N. C.   88-2-8311 and 88-86433

4. Terry Sanford, Governor
   Governor's Mansion
   Raleigh, N. C.

5. Berl I. Bernhard
   Civil Rights Commission
   Washington, D. C.

6. Robert Kennedy, Attorney General
   The Justice Department
   Washington, D. C.

7. John F. Kennedy, President
   White House
   Washington, D. C.

APPENDIX III

James McMillan, Art Professor, Bennett College, Oct 20, 2011 Interview with Linda Beatrice Brown

"Dr. David Jones hired me and gave me the inspiration to be the best I could be. I left, went to Paris, and returned to Bennett in 1961. There were expatriates at Bennett from Europe thanks to Dr. Willa Player. Those people knew about oppression. Dr. Elizabeth Laizner was one of those. She was my neighbor and I got to know her background as a victim of the holocaust.

Art students began to be involved making posters and signs. This was something we were all concerned about. I was arrested three times at the Howard Johnson's and afterwards. When Jesse Jackson was leading marches I became involved in daily marches. I remember a big march. Jesse asked me and Dr. Laizner to be leaders of the group at Dudley St. and East Market. Huge numbers of people marched in the rain. Crowds taunted us. As we got up near the square someone flashed a switch blade knife at me and Dr. Laizner. I whispered at her to keep walking. People sat-in on the street. Many townspeople sat down including my father.

I got a call from Dr. Player after the arrests and they had separated Dr. Laizner from the Bennett girls. I went to the Polio hospital and she wasn't there or in the Greensboro jail. In the High Point jail they took me downstairs. They had put Dr. Laizner in a cold cell with drunken women.

This period influenced my painting. My life's work is tied up to the injustice I saw in my community. It stimulated social statement paintings. I was mentally and emotionally involved.

"There ought to be a woman on that statue at A&T."

Dr. Julianne Malveaux, President Emerita, Bennett College, Interview with Linda Beatrice Brown, Oct 28, 2011

Brown: As someone who is not from here, what is your perception of Greensboro as a city?

Malveaux: My perception of Greensboro is that it is a city with a divided mind. The perception of Greensboro as a "nice-nasty" town has not completely changed. The Community Foundation and Action Greensboro are prepared to challenge the status quo. The fact that we had Yvonne Johnson as Mayor was important. But there are still challenges.

Brown: Why is it important to tell the story of the Sit-ins again?

Malveaux: Because history belongs to she who has the pen, and we have been self effacing....the story needs to be told. What was amazing was the resistance. We need a sense of the roles women have played whether we start with Maggie Walker, or Harriet Tubman or Dorothy Height. The baton has been passed. Our challenges are both more complex and more simple. I am a strong civil rights advocate. My record speaks to the way I encourage the students to be activists. We don't face the legal challenges they faced. We follow the history that they made challenging the law.

Brown: Do you have a message to the Belles of yesterday who participated in the movement?

Malveaux: My message is: I love you. They are the foremothers that I dreamed of. Your parents did not send you to college to Sit-in. You had to shatter the boundaries of ladyhood.

Brown: What do you want the Bennett students of today to get from this book?

<u>Malveaux:</u> I want the students at Bennett to know more about this history and to understand the multiplicity of who we are. The Sit-in Belles shattered the stereotypes. Redefinition was happening all over the city. I say look at the women who came before you and understand, you don't even know what you will do in your future.

.

APPENDIX IV
LETTERS AND CLIPPINGS

Edward Edmonds to Greensboro Daily News Supporting the NAACP , October 5, 1957

Voice of The People

DEFENDING NAACP

Editor, The Record:

With reference to your editorial appearing Oct. 1, concerning the National Association for the Advancement of Colored People, we are deeply disturbed at your labeling the organization and its leadership "extremists." For certainly this label can only be valid if an extremist, as opposed to actions of moderation, is one who seeks to obtain those rights guaranteed all Americans by the Constitution and legal precedents. Unlike many organizations of a different ilk, no one can state truthfully that the NAACP has ever resorted to anything other than persuasion, conference, and as a last resort, legal action to attain its desired ends—first class citizenship for all.

The term "moderation" is a highly respected term, and hence is most desirable as a label under which to operate. However, an examination of the facts might lead to question of the accuracy in the use of such a label for your position.

Let not your readers ever forget that, almost without exception, everything the socalled moderates now support as desirable has come through no action on their part. What voice of the "moderate" was heard pleading for justice for Negro children in educational opportunity unhampered by the stigma and inequalties of segregation prior to the successful litigation by the NAACP? What effort was made by the "moderates" to secure the rights of Negroes as American citizens in voting, in interstate and intra-state travel, in city bus riding, in the use of the city library prior to the efforts made by the NAACP?

In short, the position of "moderation" seems to be that of accepting that which cannot be helped, while at the same time decrying any efforts directed toward the effecting of further change.

Let not your readers forget that the concern you express for the losses to Negroes which may result from continuing to seek their full rights as American citizens is predicated upon the necessity of maintaining their present very circumscribed area of second class citizenship. We say to you, and to all members of the majority group, that we seek that which is rightfully ours —rights civil, and which make you poorer not one iota. Only those stand to lose who are exploiting the victims of segregation. Where is the sense of justice, of fair play, which itself is a very strong and respected tradition of the American heritage?

Let not your readers forge that your equating the NAACP with the rapid segregationist is both inaccurate and unfair to say the least. We hope that this was not a deliberate effort to smear, but rather a statement made because of a lack of knowledge of existing pertinent facts.

The National Association for the Advancement of Colored People is a legitimate, respectable organization composed of law-abiding citizens of both groups. There is not one single instance on record of it having used means other than peaceful persuasion and resort to the courts. We condemn practices of violence and terrorization. Regrettably, the same cannot be said of many of the arch segregationist groups.

We make no pretense of speaking for all Negroes in this community, no more than your paper, or the chamber of commerce speaks for the entire majority group. We speak only for our membership. However, in a democracy such as ours we have the same right to seek change as any other legally constituted group, be it church, lodge or business association.

It is our feeling that a great deal of the difficulty lies in the inability of the people to get the different sides of the problem. We would welcome opportunities to discuss our views with other groups sincerely interested in seeking solutions. Perhaps your paper could be instrumental in helping to achieve some such possibilities.

E. R. EDMONDS,
President,
Greensboro Branch, National Association for Advancement of Colored People

Willa Player Cancels Her Account

August 4, 1960   COPY

Meyer's Department Store
Greensboro
North Carolina

       Attention: Mrs. Gladys Miller
                  Second Floor, Front

My dear Mrs. Miller:

We did not have an opportunity to call you to
let you know that my account at Meyer's has
been closed. At the present time I do not con-
template opening the account. I will, therefore,
not expect to come into the store until the
policies have been changed completely.

Thank you very much for your past services. I
hope that there will come a time when the relationship may be restored.

With sincere good wishes, I am

                 Very truly yours,

                 Willa B. Player
                 President

Meyer's Acts Today
Firm Integrates Counter

A downtown department store early this afternoon was to become the fourth firm in Greensboro to begin serving food to Negroes on a sit-down basis.

Meyer's Department Store was scheduled to open its fountain shop to Negroes about 2 p.m. The firm's Garden Room was not affected in the change.

Meyer's, which sells Negroes merchandise at other counters in the store but previously had not served them on a sit-down basis at the fountain shop, altered its policy one week after two Greensboro variety stores decided to open their lunch counters to Negroes on the same basis as white customers. At mid-week a dairy bar followed their lead.

The policy changes were voluntary actions on the part of the firms involved, following a series of conferences with Negro leaders.

The departure from earlier custom has been accomplished here without incident.

Lois Lucas Letter to Greensboro Daily News

GREENSBORO DAILY NEWS
Sunday, October 23, 1962
Letters to the Editor

In both the news broadcast and he article carried by the Daily News, it was stated that "A white nan once convicted as a member f the Communist Party and his vife have been sent to Greensoro as representatives of the Communist Party to assist stulents of two Negro colleges here n efforts to break racial barriers n restaurants and other commercial establishments."

I should like to ask a simple question directed towards Attorney Armistead Sapp Jr.. who made he charge. What proof does he lave that would substantiate such a charge? Can he prove beyond a loubt that these persons were 'sent to Greensboro as representatives of the Communist Party"? f he cannot do this then I feel hat a retraction is in order.

I feel that a public apology is lue to the Bennett College community. Attorney A. Sapp, Jr., las no valid evidence that would support his personal viewpoint hat the "mass demonstration was omented by the Communists." This statement was made on the news broadcast. Nor can the implied connection with the Black Muslim movement be substantiated. Just what does Attorney Sapp mean when he uses the ad- jective substantial in connection with the number of students at A&T and Bennett who allegedly may be Communist? There is an implication of knowledge that would support the adjective in question. Can this implication be either clarified or proven beyond doubt?

Since Attorney Sapp is concerned with the public being kept up to date on the current activities of C.O.R.E. and the character of the people who participate I should like to add to the general information. Leaders of C.O.R.E have been threatened unless their work is stopped in the field of civil rights.

Articles and news broadcasts that are filled with unfounded implications aimed at smearing an individual or an institution degrade even the media of communication upon which it is made known. This is especially true when these implications have as their final goal the dissolution of the forces which work to make democracy feasible for all Americans.

I should like for Attorney Sapp to either substantiate or retract his implications. This substantiation should have been the first fact given to the public in view of the alleged concern for the awareness of the public.

I feel sure that Attorney Sapp's concern will not let him misinform the public. So I therefore challenge Attorney Sapp to prove his impli cations.

Lois Lucas, Bennett College

APPENDIX V
PHOTOGRAPHS

Massive March Led By
Bennett Professor Elizabeth Laizner, Jesse Jackson, and James McMillan

(Daily News staff photo

LEADING THE MARCH
Jesse Jackson (left) president of student government at A&T College, leads demonstrators on a peaceful march through down town Greensboro. In the center is Dr. Elizabeth Leizner, a teacher at Bennett College. The Negro man at the right is unidentified *Rlin McMillan*

Bennett Student Campaigns for JFK in Greensboro
Gwendolyn Mackel Rice '61

Photo: Courtesy of Gwendolyn Mackel Rice

Bennett Students Arrested for Sitting-In
April 1960

Students Charged with Trespassing

On April 22, 1960 forty-five A & T and Bennett students were arrested on warrants charging them with trespass at the S. H. Kress & Co. lunch counter. "I remember some fear, but also a great deal of courage," Gwen Mackel-Rice, class of '61, emphasized. "It was something we knew we had to do . . . .I had grown up in a family where 'this is the order of the day.' Before I was born, my parents fought for improved classrooms for the black students in Monroe, Louisiana. This was a part of our life. We didn't ride in the back of the bus. We had to walk or wait until someone could drive us where we needed to go. We did not say 'Yes, Sir' and 'Yes, Ma'am' and 'No, Sir' to white people. We were taught not to" (Mackel-Rice 1996 14)

Left to Right Ann Brown, Sandra Downing, Shirley Dismuke, Mary Ellen Bender

Text: Courtesy of Barbara Isaacs

Photo: Courtesy of Greensboro News and Record

Negro Marchers Signal Boycott of Merchants, 1963

1,500 March; Integration Requested

An estimated 1,500 N e g r o e s paraded silently t h r o u g h the downtown section of Greensboro yesterday afternoon in a demonstration described as the beginning of a "selective buying campaign" directed a g a i n s t merchants in an effort to integrate restaurants, hotels and movie houses.

A spokesman said that all students at Bennett and A&T Colleges and other members of the Negro community had been asked to participate. The march, in which participants walked in single file on sidewalks, began about 2:15 p.m. and continued over a pre-determined route for about one hour. It was sponsored by local units of CORE and NAACP.

The spokesman said that "pressure (against merchants) will be applied until favorable results are reached." Police described the demonstration as orderly. "It was a very well behaved' group and caused no trouble at all," said Major Howard Wooters. The mid-town area was saturated with officers who were alerted in advance of the demonstration.

See Photo Next Page

Bennett's Elsie Jacobs and Other Students
March
In Greensboro, 1963

(Daily News staff photo

NEGRO MARCHERS SIGNAL BOYCOTT OF MERCHANTS
At first sight as they appeared on East Market Street, they seemed to come in endless numbers. Later, police estimated the "silent marchers" at some 1,500, most of them college students. They walked in single file through downtown Greensboro yesterday afternoon for about one hour in an incident-free demonstraion to mark the beginning of a "selective buying campaign" against merchants. A spokesman for CORE and the NAACP, the sponsoring groups, said "pressure" against merchants will continue until restaurants, hotels and movie houses are integrated.

Photo: Courtesy of Greensboro News and Record

Sit In Demonstration by Bennett Women
And Others at Woolworth Store

Photo: Courtesy of Greensboro News and Record

Bennett Student Mary Ellen Bender
And Others Picket
Downtown Greensboro Businesses

Photo: Courtesy of Greensboro Daily News

Bennett Student Ollie Johnson Pickets
Downtown Greensboro

Photo: Courtesy of Greensboro News and Record

Greensboro Police Surround Students
And Citizens, June 1963

Police surround the crowd at a student march at Jefferson Square in Greensboro in June, 1963. The demonstrations which ultimately helped desegregate all downtown businesses, were led by A&T student leader Jesse Jackson, who came to Greensboro in the wake of the 1960 Woolworth Sit-ins.

Photo: Courtesy of Greensboro News and Record
Text: Chafe, *Civilities and Civil Rights*

Greensboro Daily News   Monday April 4, 1960

WEATHER

Mild; Scattered Showers
Expected High Today, 70
TEMPERATURES YESTERDAY
High, 60; Low, 48
(Other Data, Page 1, Section B)

VOL. XCVII, No. 79

Over 1,000 Hear Negro Leader

Marshall Urges Segregation End

(Daily News staff photo.)

BEFORE SPEECH
Thurgood Marshall, general counsel for the NAACP, stands with Bennett College student Gloria McKnight of Gainesville, Fla., before he spoke at the opening of the school's annual Homemaking Institute.

The general counsel of the National Association for the Advancement of Colored People yesterday described Southern aristocracy as the "white man's right to sit at a lunch counter and drink a 10-cent cup of coffee."

Thurgood Marshall made the remark to an audience of more than 1,000 Negroes at the opening of Bennett College's Homemaking Institute.

Urging his audience to provide their own leadership in putting an end to all segregation, Marshall said "the world will never condone oppression of minorities no matter who's on top and who's on bottom.

"The only country that doesn't understand this is the United States," he said.

Not Private

Marshall said he didn't think much of last week's suggestion by the mayor's committee that partial integration of dime store lunch counters here would solve the problem brought on by Negro student demands for an end to segregated seating.

NAACP Leader Urges End To Segregation

Marshall was asked what he thought of the statement by some Southerners that the cause of better race relations had been set back by the wave of student sit-down demonstrations.

"People throughout the country are demonstrating their support for it," he said. "Besides, I have never understood what they mean by 'setting back' race relations."

The Negro lawyer planned to return to New York City last night. The Bennett College homemaking institute continues this week with an effort by students to get Negro residents to register to vote.

BIBLIOGRAPHY

"Adults Warned to Be Prepared to Go to Jail." Greensboro Daily News 20 May 1963: B1.

"Air of Calmness Hanging Over Jammed Old Polio Hospital." Greensboro Record 20 May 1963: B1.

"Ann Dearsley Reviews Lunch Counter Strike." Carolinian 12 Feb 1960.

Bates, Gerri. "These Hallowed Halls: African American Women College And University Presidents." The Journal of Negro Education 76 (2007).

Bennett, Lerone. Great Moments in Black History. Chicago: Johnson Publishing Co., 1979.

"Bennett Students Doorknock for Voters Paid Off." Digitalnc.org Bennett College scrapbook 1 July, 1961.

Blackwell, Gordon William. "Chancellor Blackwell's Speech to WCUNC Students Regarding the Greensboro Sit-ins". Civil Rights Greensboro library.uncg.edu.

Blassingame, John W. "The Revolution that Never Was: the Civil Rights Movement 1950-1980." Perspectives 2.14 (1982).

Brandon, Lewis III. "The Era of the Sit-ins: Greensboro, NC" unpublished papers, 1995.

Brandon, Lewis III. "The Greening of the A&T Four and the February 1st Movement." Feb 2001: unpublished monograph.

Breines, Winifred. Rev. Of Gender and the Civil Rights Movement, Peter J. Ling, and Sharon Monteith and Throwing off the Cloak of White Privilege; White Southern Women Activists in the Civil Rights Era Gail S. Murray. Signs 4.31 (Summer 2006): 1164-1167.

Brown, Carolyn. "A Nation Worries, A Campus Studies." Bennett Banner, Feb. 1958, digitalnc.org.

Brown, Flora Bryant. "NAACP Sponsored Sit-ins by Howard University Students in Washington, DC." Journal of Negro History 4.85 (Autumn 2000): 274-286.

Brown, Linda Beatrice. The Long Walk: The Story of the Presidency of Willa Player at Bennett College. Danville, Virginia: McCain Printing, 1998.

Caplan, Marvin Harold. Farther Along: A Civil Rights Memoir. Baton Rouge: Louisiana State University Press, 1999.

Chafe, William Henry. The American Woman 1920-1970. New York: Oxford University Press, 1974.

_____. Civilities and Civil Rights: Greensboro NC and the Black Struggle for Freedom. New York: Oxford University Press, 1981.

_____. The Civil Rights Movement. Ed. Ogbar, Jeffrey O.G. Boston; Houghton Mifflin, 2003.

_____. Interview with Hobart Jarrett. 1975 <http://library.uncg.edu/intv4.23.652 Repository Duke University. http:www.aas.duke.edu.

Cheagle, Roslyn. "Where Do You Stand." Bennett Banner 1959, digitalnc.org. Civil Rights Greensboro. The University Libraries, Greensboro, NC. 2 Feb. 2012. http://library.uncg.edu.

"Civil Rights Movement" The Reader's Companion.
http://www.credoreference.com.

Cole, Johnnetta Betsch, and Beverly Guy Scheftall. Gender Talk.
New York: Ballantine Books, 2003.

"Colleges Ponder Student Problem." Greensboro Record 21 May
1963: B1.

Collier-Thomas, Bettye, and Franklin, V.P. editors. Sisters in the
Struggle: African American Women in the Civil Rights-Black
Power Movement. New York; New York University Press, 2001.

"Conditions of 'Jail' Cited." Greensboro Daily News 20 May
1963: B1.

Cozzens, Lisa. "The Montgomery Bus Boycott" 28 June 1998
http://watson.org/nlisa/Black history/civilrights-55-65/
montbus.html.

"Demonstrators March Again, Anti Segregation Demonstrations
Continued." Greensboro Daily News 19 May 1963:16.

"Demonstrators March Again 287 Arrested." Greensboro Daily
News 19 May 1963: A 1.

"Desegregation of Greensboro Businesses 1962-63" Civil Rights
Greensboro, library.uncg.edu. The University Libraries
Greenbsoro, NC.

Farrington, Thomas. "A Night in the Pen." A&T Register 29
May 1963: 2.

"400 [Four-hundred] Arrested in Demonstration Here."
Greensboro Daily News 18 May 1963: A1.

"Fifty Years Since the Civil Rights Sit-ins." Randolph-Macon
Woman's College Alumnae and Randolph College Alumni
Bulletin Fall 2010: 8-14.

Flowers, Deidre B. "The Launching of the Student Sit-in Movement: The Role of Black Women at Bennett College." The Journal of African American History, 90.1,2. Source: Brown v Board of Education: Fifty Years of Educational Change in the United States, 2004" (Winter 2005) 52-63.

Franklin, V.P. "Patterns of Students Activism at Historically Black Universities in the US and South Africa 1860-1977," The Journal of African American History 2.88. Source: The History of Student Activism (Spring 2003) 204-217.

Frystak, Shannon H. Our Minds on Freedom : Women in the Struggle for Black Equality in Louisiana 1924-1967. Baton Rouge: Louisiana State University Press, 2009.

Giddings, Paula. "A Legacy of the 60's: Education, Race, and Reality." Source: Change 2.22 (March April, 1990), 10-17.

Green, Laurie B. Battling the Plantation Mentality: Memphis and the Black Freedom Struggle. Chapel Hill: University of NC Press, 2007.

"Greater Race Problem: Understanding Aim of Mt. Holyoke Exchange." Digitalnc.org. Bennett College scrapbook 17 Feb. 1961.

Gyant, La Verne. "Passing the Torch; African American Women in the Civil Rights Movement." Journal of Black Studies 5.26 (May 1996) 629-647.

Hatchett, John. "Hidden From History: Bennett College Women and the Greensboro Sit-ins." Freedom Socialist 1.26 (Feb.-March 2005) 2-4.

Hatchett, John. Interview with Eugene Pfaff. Keep on Walkin' Keep On Talkin'. Greensboro: Tudor Publishers, 2011.

Hawkins, Karen and Cat McDowell. "Desegregation of Greensboro Businesses 1962-1963." Civil Rights Greensboro.

The University Libraries. Greensboro, NC 12 April, http//uncg.edu.

Hine, Darlene Clark, ed. The State of Afro-American History: Past Present and Future. Baton Rouge: Louisiana State University Press, 1986.

Isaacs, Barbara Ruth Irene. The Lunch Counter Struggle 1960-1963 Women Re-mapping Boundaries of Race, Gender and Vocation. Diss Northwestern University, 2002. Evanston, Illinois.

James, Carolyn. "As I See It." Bennett Banner Nov 1960: 2.

Khazan, Jibreel. Interview with Eugene Pfaff Jr. 1979, Keep on Walkin' Keep On Talkin': An Oral History of the Greensboro Civil Rights Movement. Greensboro: Tudor Press, 2011.

Kerr, Lane. "White Girls from Mass. End Study at Negro College Here." Greensboro Daily News 26 Feb 1961: A20. digitalnc.org Bennett College scrapbook.

King, Martin Luther Jr. MLK-kppo1 Stanford.edu/.../ 11 Feb-1958, Interview at Bennett College.pdf.

Lawson, Steven F. "Freedom Then, Freedom Now: the Historiography of the Civil Rights Movement." American Historical Review 2.96 (April, 1991) 456-471.

Ling, Peter J. "A Question of Leadership." Rev. of "How Long," Belinda Hobnett. Source: Reviews in American History 2.27 (June, 1999) 289-297. Ling, Peter J. and Sharon Monteith, eds. Gender and the Civil Rights Movement, New Brunswick: Rutgers University Press, 2004.

Malveaux, Julianne. Personal interview with Linda Beatrice Brown. 28 Oct, 2011.

"Mass Move Conducted by Negroes." Greensboro Daily News 16 May 1963: A1.

Mays, Benjamin. "Creative Living for Youth in a Time of Crisis," The Bennett College Social Justice Lecture Series. 1 (Fall, 1998): 23.

McGuire, Danielle. "It Was Like All of Us Had Been Raped: Sexual Violence, Community Mobilization and the African American Freedom Struggle." The Journal of American History 3.91 (Dec. 2004) 906-931.

McKinney, Charles Wesley. The Evolution of the Civil Rights Struggle in Wilson, NC. Lanham, Maryland: University Press of America, 2010.

McMillan, James. Personal interview with Linda Beatrice Brown. 20 Oct 2011.

"Merchants Call for Integration." Greensboro Record 16 May 1963: A1.

"Montgomery Pastor Emphasizes Additional Responsibilities of New Order." Bennett Banner Feb. 1958: XXV no. 6.

Morris, Alden. "Black Southern Student Sit-In Movement: An Analysis of Internal Organization." American Sociological Review 6.16 (December 1981) 744-764.

"Movement by Negroes Growing," Greensboro Daily News 4 Feb. 1960: B.

"Negroes March Again." Greensboro Daily News 25 May 1963: np.

Ogbar, Jeffrey O.G. ed., The Civil Rights Movement. Boston: Houghton Mifflin, 2003.

Oppenheimer, Martin. The Sit-In Movement of 1960. Brooklyn, New York: Carlson Publishing Inc., 1989.

Oppenheimer, Martin. "The Southern Student Movement: Year I." The Journal of Negro Education. 4.33 (Autumn, 1964) 396-403.

Payne, Charles. I've Got the Light of Freedom: The Organizing Tradition and the Mississippi Freedom Struggle. Berkley: The University of California Press, 1995.

Payne, Justin (interviewer) Anne Bisher (interviewee) The University Libraries, Civil Rights Greensboro. library.uncg.edu oral history 28 Oct 2008.

Pfaff, Eugene E. Jr. Keep on Walkin' Keep on Talkin': An Oral History Of The Greensboro Civil Rights Movement, Greensboro: Tudor Publishers, 2011.

Player, Willa. Interview with Eugene Pfaff. 3 Dec 1979, Keep on Walkin' Keep on Talkin'.

Rice, Gwendolyn. Interview with Carmen Smith and T. Jeffries. 9 Feb 2010. Sit-In Profile interview, Bennett College.

Robnett, Belinda. "African American Women in the Civil Rights Movement 1954-1965: Gender Leadership and Micromobilization." The American Journal of Sociology 6.101 (May 1996): 1661-1693.

_____"How Long? How Long? African American Women in the Struggle for Civil Rights. New York: Oxford University Press, 1997.

Scher, D. (interviewer) and Revell Y. (interviewee): (2004). Yvonne Revell: Civil Rights Movement [interview transcript] Retrieved From the John Novak Digital Interview Collection of the Marygrove College Library web site: http:// research. Marygrove.edu novak interviews/index.html.

Scher, D. and Rice, G.M. (interviewee): (2011). Gwendolyn Mackel Rice: Civil Rights Movement [interview transcript] Retrieved from John Novak Digital Interview Collection of the Marygrove College Library web site: http://research.marygrove.edu novak interviews/index.html.

_____ and Smith R (interviewee): (2011). Roslyn Smith: Civil Rights Movement [interview transcript]. Retrieved from the John Novak Digital Interview Collection of the Marygrove College Library web site: http://research.marygrove.edu/novakintervie/index.html.

_____ and Terry E (interviewee): (2010). Esther Terry: Civil Rights Movement [interview transcript]. Retrieved form the John Novak Digital Interview Collection of the Marygrove College Library web site:http://research.marygrove.edu/novakinterviews/index.html.

Seamans, Eugenia Mark. Interview with Herman J. Trojanowski. 17 June 2007 (qtd in: Pfaff, Eugene, Keep on Walkin' Keep on Talkin').

Sharp, Sandra Echols. "We're Still Marching." The Greensboro Gazette Oct 1997: 6-7.

Simkins, George. Interview with Jim Schlosser. n.d. (qtd in: Pfaff, Eugene, Keep on Walkin' Keep on Talkin').

Smith, Roslyn. Personal interview with Linda Beatrice Brown. 31 Oct., 2011.

Stanley, A. Knighton. Interview with Eugene Pfaff 26 Jan, 1982, Keep on Walkin' Keep on Talkin'. Greensboro: Tudor Press, 2011.

Terry, Esther. Personal interview with Linda Beatrice Brown. 31 Oct. 2011.

Tisdale, Geneva. Interview with Jim Schlosser. 1998 (qtd in: Pfaff, Eugene Jr., Keep on Walkin' Keep on Talkin').

Toth, Elizabeth. Interview with Herman J. Trojanowski. 2007
(qtd in: Pfaff, Eugene Jr, <u>Keep on Walkin' Keep on Talkin'</u>).

"Trespassing Trials Begin Here." <u>A&T Register</u> 29 May, 1963:
XXIV 30.

Ward, Audrey. Unpublished Oral History Project. Bennett
College, 1997-98.

Walters, Ronald. "Standing Up in America's Heartland."
<u>American Visions</u>: Feb/March 1993: 20-23.

Wilson, Karen Leach. "The Negro's Stand." <u>Greensboro Daily
News</u> 8 Feb 1960: public pulse page.

Wolff, Miles. <u>Lunch at the 5&10</u>. Chicago: Elephant Paperbacks,
1970.

INDEX

ABOUT THE AUTHOR

Linda Beatrice Brown has taught at Kent State University, UNC-Greensboro and Guilford College. A graduate of Bennett College, she is presently the Willa B. Player Distinguished Professor of the Humanities at Bennett College where until this year she taught African American Literature. She is the author of three novels, *Rainbow 'Roun Mah Shoulder*, *Crossing Over Jordan* and *Black Angels*.

Linda usually writes about the African American experience. She is also a poet and has been a guest lecturer at many schools, colleges and in different cities throughout the country. She has poetry in several anthologies and magazines.

Plays include *Wildfire: Black Hands White Marble*, the story of Edmonia Lewis a Black Indian sculptor who broke historical barriers with her art, performed in both Greensboro and Winston Salem; *Kitchen Talk* performed at Bennett College; *Stop Right There and Let Me Tell You About My Children*, the story of Harriet Jacobs, a slave in hiding, also performed at Bennett. Her play *Congo's River Song* was produced by the NC Museum of Art. Linda's novel *Black Angels* was the "Okra Pick" for the 2009 annual conference of South Carolina Independent booksellers and was named one of the best books of 2009 by the Chicago Public Libraries.

Belles of Liberty grew out of Linda's lifelong conviction that she has a responsibility to speak out for justice and equality. For many years she was a diversity trainer for the Episcopal Church. A member of the choir at Holy Trinity Episcopal Church, Linda also sings with the Spiritual Renaissance Singers of Greensboro. She has two adult children, six grandchildren and is now at work on a sequel to her novel *Black Angels*. She lives with her husband, Gerald White, in Greensboro.

CONTACT INFORMATION

WWW.LINDABEATRICEBROWN.COM

WWW.WOMENANDWISDOM.COM